Handbook of Field Methods
for Monitoring Landbirds

C. John Ralph   Geoffrey R. Geupel   Peter Pyle   Thomas E. Martin   David F. DeSante

Contents

Contents

In Brief . . .

Ralph, C. John; Geupel, Geoffrey R.; Pyle, Peter; Martin, Thomas E.; DeSante, David F. 1993. **Handbook of field methods for monitoring landbirds.** Gen. Tech. Rep. PSW-GTR-144. Albany, CA: Pacific Southwest Research Station, Forest Service, U.S. Department of Agriculture; 41 p.

Retrieval Terms: bird populations, census, mist-nets, monitoring, nesting birds

The increased attention devoted to the status and possible declines of populations of smaller species of terrestrial birds, known collectively as "landbirds," has resulted in an immediate need for specific methodology for monitoring their populations. This handbook is derived from several sources and is based on the authors' collective experiences in operating monitoring stations. Presented here are a compilation of methods that can be used to assay population size, demographics, and status of virtually all species of landbirds in a wide variety of habitats, from grassland and tundra to temperate and tropical rain forests. Rare species, or those with unusual habits, will require some modifications. The handbook will prove useful to field biologists, managers, and scientists anywhere in the New World. The handbook first suggests priorities for selecting a monitoring method and determining station locations. Then, general tasks that determine which species can be monitored, and methods of establishing and maintaining a study plot, journal keeping, and training of personnel are presented. Two demographic methods are described, one involving mist nets, and the other finding nests during the breeding season. Detailed suggestions are given for both methods which should allow a trained person to successfully operate a station. Both methods involve monitoring at a station at regular intervals during the breeding season. The handbook also includes descriptions of four types of censuses for determining population size and trends: spot mapping of territories, area searches of specific sites, strip transects along predetermined routes, and point counts. The latter method has been accepted as the standard method, is treated in most detail, and involves a person standing in one spot for 3 to 10 minutes and recording all birds seen or heard. In addition, methods are suggested for measuring habitat, recording weather, and color-banding individuals to determine specific demographic parameters. Throughout the handbook, sources of materials are given that are needed for each method, as well as specific references to published works.

USDA Forest Service Gen. Tech. Rep. PSW-GTR-144-www. 1993.

iii

Introduction

Throughout the New World attention is now being focused on the status of populations of landbirds, which are the many species of smaller birds, sometimes referred to as "non-game" birds. Landbirds have not usually been the focus of management activities except in a few cases of threatened or endangered species, such as the Kirtland's Warbler. Recent evidence suggests that some landbird species are declining in abundance, fueling much speculation upon the causes of these declines, the species involved, and their habitat preferences. Hypotheses about the causes of these declines are varied, ranging from tropical deforestation to nest parasitism by the cowbird. However, part of the difficulty in determining the status of landbirds results from problems in monitoring these small birds, as compared to larger, more easily-studied species. To determine population changes, and to hypothesize possible causes of these changes, more basic information needs to be gathered.

Much of the evidence for these population declines in the New World has come from the results of the Breeding Bird Survey coordinated by the U.S. Fish and Wildlife Service and the Canadian Wildlife Service (Robbins and others 1986, 1989). These roadside counts provide excellent baseline data. However, they do little to identify the factors contributing to changes in landbird populations, and are limited to areas with major roads.

The use of population size as a measure of health of a species has been a common tool of biologists for many years (Hutchinson 1978; Lack 1954, 1966). Methods for surveying population size have been detailed by Ralph and Scott (1981), in the excellent compendium by Cooperrider and others (1986), and the manual by Koskimies and Vaisanen (1991). Population size, however, is only a retrospective tool. It tells only after the fact that a species has enjoyed an increase or suffered a decline. To ponder causes of changes, the biologist must couple information on population size with data on the internal composition of a population—its demographics (Temple and Wiens 1989). For example, data on sex ratio, age distribution, nesting success, survivorship, average weight, and population movements can all give valuable cues to factors or events regulating a population. Moreover, such primary population characters can provide early warning signals of population problems prior to actual declines. Many studies have used data such as these to describe the dynamics of various populations (DeSante and Geupel 1987, Hutchinson 1978).

Several other efforts have been under way to document changes in adult populations and in productivity. For example, in the late 1970's, the Germans and Austrians started the "Mettnau-Reit-Illmitz-Programm" (Berthold and Scherner 1975). Since 1981, the British Trust for Ornithology has conducted their Constant Effort Sites (CES) Scheme (Baillie and others 1986; Baillie and Holden 1988;

Peach and Baillie 1991; Peach and others 1991). Martin has started a program involving nest searches (Martin and Geupel in press). DeSante (1991, 1992a,b) has started a cooperative mist-netting program in North America known as "Monitoring Avian Productivity and Survivorship" (MAPS) along these same lines. The Point Reyes Bird Observatory has been monitoring landbird populations in coastal California for more than 25 years (Ralph 1967, Geupel and DeSante 1990b).

In this handbook we outline the steps that might be followed in monitoring many species of landbirds. We cover methods used in monitoring of population size, productivity, age and sex ratios, survivorship, habitat relationships, and other parameters. We provide details of four methods that estimate population size, two methods that measure demographic factors, and two suggestions for conducting habitat assessment. We have tried to give the land manager, biologist, and others complete information on basic requirements, tools, resources, and methods to carry out a successful landbird monitoring program. Depending on funding and staffing, any combination of the techniques we describe is applicable to virtually any site and budget. This handbook does not provide the objectives of each study that might be conducted, or what analyses can be conducted. These both must be examined carefully before monitoring begins. We hope that this handbook will generate interest in monitoring programs using methods that can give insight into causes, as well as the facts, of population changes.

Objectives of a Monitoring Program

A monitoring program ideally should provide three types of data. One is an estimate of the population size and trends for various species of birds. The second is an estimate of the demographic parameters for at least some of those populations. The third is habitat data to link the density and demographic parameters of bird populations to habitat characteristics. Ideally a monitoring program should take a community approach and monitor all avian species in the area.

We have recently seen a marked increase in interest in monitoring, far outstripping available personnel, training, and resources. Indeed, this increase is the impetus for this handbook. While this has been gratifying, we think that it is essential that people first determine why they might want to establish a census, mist netting, or nest searching program. Not everyone requires a monitoring program to meet their goals. We have sometimes seen the establishment of a monitoring program first, followed by an attempt to decide what type of information can be obtained. We very strongly suggest that, before a monitoring program is put in place, the following steps be carried out: (1) decide the objectives and goals desired; (2) determine whether monitoring is the way to accomplish these; (3) with the goals firmly in mind, write down the questions being asked, clearly and objectively; (4) determine which monitoring methods most directly answer the questions posed; (5) review the types of data that can be obtained from these methods, and outline exactly how these data will answer the questions; (6) outline the analytical methods that can be employed; (7) determine the cost, logistics, availability of personnel, and probable length of commitment to the project; and (8) write a study plan and have it reviewed by a person competent in research and statistics. This procedure is vital, because accumulation of a data base does not itself lead to meaningful analyses later.

Participants in a monitoring program can include private, state, provincial, and federal groups. Our premise is that the basic entity for this exercise is an administrative unit, such as a Forest Service District or a State Park. Not all such units will want or need such a program. Each unit should outline its needs and goals before starting, suggest monitoring programs to meet those needs, and have them reviewed by a competent biostatistician. We do believe, however, that our recommendations below have generality among many types of administrative units. These units can be very heterogeneous, and thus a variety of methods may be needed.

Glossary

Landbirds: the general term used for the generally smaller birds (usually exclusive of raptors and upland game birds) not usually associated with aquatic habitats. By contrast, waterbirds include seabirds and other aquatic species.

Region: an area of several thousand acres, often including several drainages, that the biologist wishes to sample. Here, extensive point counts are conducted on roads to monitor overall population sizes and their changes.

Administrative unit: the basic entity that conducts monitoring. Examples are a Forest Service District or Forest, a State Park, a National Wildlife Refuge, a private nature center, or a commercial forest.

Monitoring station: an area of usually less than about 50 ha (125 acres) within a region. Here, intensive censuses, nest searching, and mist netting are conducted.

Capture array: the generally rectangular or circular configuration of mist net locations at a station.

Nest search or census plot: an area of, preferably, a single habitat type where spot mapping or area searches are conducted.

Census grid: the arrangement of intensive point counts overlaying a demographic mist net array or nest search plot.

Census point: the place where a single point count census is taken.

Net location: the place where a single net is placed.

Nest site: the place where a single nest is found.

A 10-day time: **interval** is the basis for most monitoring and analyses.

Selecting Monitoring Methods and Location of Monitoring Stations

Before beginning work, careful attention should be given to selecting the appropriate method for the questions being asked, and great care should be given to selecting locations of monitoring stations to best answer these questions.

Selection of Methods

The standardized set of methodologies described below should be followed closely to ensure compatibility with those of other monitoring stations. These methodologies are integrated and hierarchic, so as to allow a region's sampling schemes to complement other programs and to allow comparisons between monitoring stations in a region, and between regions.

Methods recommended should be employed for a minimum of three years, and preferably longer. However, depending on individual objectives, some results may be obtainable in a year or two.

What Will the Data from This Program Provide?

These data will be used at two geographic scales. At the level of the managed forest, for instance a large National Forest District, they will provide a local assessment of the status and trends of landbirds. The scheme below samples the landscape as a whole within the unit and will permit statements such as: "Scarlet Tanagers have significantly increased on the sampled units in the forest," "Hermit Thrushes have had high mortality during migration or the winter in the past two years," or "15 of 20 neotropical migrants have increased over the past 3 years." Such a local scheme will permit some investigation of patterns of population change (e.g., "are declining trends more prevalent in units of the northern half of the forest?", "do increasing trends appear to be associated with certain forestry practices?"). Their primary purpose, however, is to estimate the status and trends of the population. Assessment of the *cause* of population change, or associations with environmental factors such as cutting practices, are more efficiently studied by other research programs with more appropriate techniques.

At the larger scale, perhaps a Forest Service Region, a state, or a province, the program will permit evaluation of geographic patterns of various attributes of landbirds. It is important to realize that the program cannot evaluate the population status of birds of the entire geographic area, whether regional, state, federal, or continental. If, for example, samples are only from forested environments, only statements about birds using forested lands can be made. Additionally, because sites are chosen by the unit, and are not a random sample of all available units or sites, the program can investigate only the *patterns* of population change, rather than the population's overall status. Questions

2

USDA Forest Service Gen. Tech. Rep. PSW-GTR-144-www. 1993.

this approach can answer, for example, are: "are population increases or reproductive failures in a group of species more prevalent in some regions or states?"; "what is the association between forest management and population status of a group of species?"; "do some forest types have more neotropical migrants than others?"; or "are populations increasing in some forest types, but not in others?"

Coverage

While it would be best to have complete coverage of any state, province, or region, we do believe that it is acceptable and inevitable that gaps will exist. These gaps will occur within habitat types, forests, states, provinces, or regions. At a minimum, we hope to have several units involved in each state, province, or region. We strongly urge that each unit have both population and demographic methods in operation, and cover anything from a few hundred to several thousand acres. Further, we suggest that sampling within a unit should be stratified by at least general habitat type, such as "mixed coniferous forests," "tropical thorn forest," or "coastal chaparral." Samples in an analysis, in general, should not be pooled across habitat types. The data from these units would be searched for large-scale patterns, e.g., species showing consistent declines over the entire region or within a given habitat type. Results from these investigations will identify patterns that need further research or greater intensity of monitoring to determine their causes. The overall program could be considered a large-scale hypothesis-generating mechanism.

Table 1—*Census and demographic monitoring methods*

Variables and characters	Census			Demographic	
	Point count	Spot map	Area search	Mist nets	Nest search
Variables measured					
Index to abundance	yes	yes	yes	yes	partly
Density	no	yes	no	no	partly
Survivorship (adult)	no	no	no	yes	no
Survivorship (juvenile)	no	no	no	yes	partly
Productivity	no	no	no	yes	yes
Recruitment	no	no	no	yes	no
Habitat relations	yes	yes	yes	little	partly
Clutch size	no	no	no	no	yes
Predation/parasitism	no	no	no	no	yes
Individuals identified	no	no	no	yes	yes
Breeding status known	no	yes	no	partly	yes
General characters					
Habitat types measured	all	some	most	some	few
Habitat specificity	good	good	good	fair	good
Rare species measured	many	few	many	some	few
Canopy species measured	all	all	all	some	few
Area sampled known	partly	yes	yes	partly	yes
Size of area sampled	moderate	small	small	large	small
Training necessary	much	much	moderate	much	much
Observer error potential	high	high	moderate	moderate	moderate
Use in non-breeding	yes	no	yes	yes	no
Cost per data point	low	high	low	high	very high
Applicable scale	broad	local	broad	broad	local

Priorities

Methodologies are compared in *table 1*. At a minimum we recommend that the following programs of demographic and population monitoring be implemented in each unit, in the following order. Although this handbook describes three censusing methods, the point count method has been adopted as the recommended standard, and its implementation is suggested below. Each recommended method is in segments of 10 person-days, other than the first which takes one person-day. For example, if funding is available for 21 person-days of field work, then only Priorities I through III (outlined below) would be implemented. These estimates of time do not include set-up or training. These will vary depending upon qualifications of personnel. The minimum numbers of counts or netting sites, noted below, are derived from our experiences with many such population monitoring programs. We believe they are useful, but not restrictive, minima for a unit's effort.

Priority I. Breeding Bird Survey—If the unit is in North America and has an unsurveyed Fish and Wildlife Service Breeding Bird Survey route within or near it, we recommend that the standard survey be conducted. This involves 50 3-minute point counts along roads at 0.5-mile (1-km) intervals. The effort takes one person-day at the height of the breeding season, usually in early June. The surveyor must know all of the vocalizations of species likely to be encountered. This Survey will help detect regional trends in many species in the unit, or its vicinity.

Priority II. On-Road Point Counts—As a second priority, we recommend that the unit put in point-counting stations in multiples of about 250 stations to monitor overall population changes and responses to habitats. We suggest that the stations be in habitats representative of the unit, stratified by these major habitats, systematically placed, and placed primarily along secondary roads. This level of effort will require about 10 person-days during the early breeding season, usually in May or June. It is based on the assumption that in the 10-day period, an average of about 25 stations can be censused in each day. While we acknowledge the fact that an on-road monitoring program is not without bias, the benefits are considered by most workers to outweigh the disadvantages, and are at least partly offset by Priority IV, below.

Priority III. Demographic Monitoring—We recommend that the unit establish at least one site to measure demographic parameters. Either constant-effort mist netting or nest searches (both, if possible) should be conducted on usually about six plots within each unit. These monitoring stations will estimate demographic variables that influence the density estimates.

Constant-Effort Mist-Netting Sites—Operating mist nets through the breeding season, at most North American stations, will require about 10 person-days per site, beginning about June and continuing through the end of August. In Latin America, the season would be longer. The program will provide information on productivity, survivorship, and movement of many species. Mist netting involves capturing birds, banding them, and taking data on age, sex, breeding

USDA Forest Service Gen. Tech. Rep. PSW-GTR-144-www. 1993.

3

status, molt, and survivorship. At a minimum each monitoring station should operate 8-12 nets at least once every 10 days throughout the breeding season. It has become well established that results from constant-effort mist netting provide excellent indexes of productivity and recruitment for a variety of species (e.g., DeSante and Geupel 1987, Peach and others 1990, Peach 1992). It is the only method that estimates survivorship and recruitment using mark and recapture. Its major weakness is that the recruitment data are not habitat specific, especially late in the summer. The survivorship data are excellent, and all data are most habitat specific for adults, especially early in the breeding season. As the season progresses, influx of peripheral birds and young from other areas dilutes this specificity.

Nest Searching Sites—Nest searches involve intensively finding nests in a plot. Typically, one plot can be done in about 20-40 person-days, beginning about May and continuing to about August. Nest searching involves finding nests, monitoring their outcome, and measuring associated vegetation. A study plot needs to be visited at least once every four days to find and check nests. Nest searches provide direct measures of reproductive success (rather than an index) and can provide direct data on influences of habitat on reproductive success and the incidence of nest parasitism. Nest searching, however, is quite labor intensive and is applicable to fewer species than mist netting.

A drawback to both demographic methods is that they will assay the population health of only certain species in an area. As a general rule of thumb, usually about 10 species at any one station will be monitored. However, when data from several stations are combined over a larger geographical area, meaningful insights may be gained on many species.

In addition, within each demographic plot, at least 9-16 intensive point count censuses should be conducted at least twice during the peak of the breeding season. Other census methods (i.e., spot mapping, area search) may also be employed, depending on objectives, size of study area, and availability of personnel. Vegetation measures should also be made at each census point and within each demographic plot.

Priority IV. Off-Road Point Counts—As a fourth priority, we recommend that the unit conduct point counts in segments of approximately 100 points off-roads in habitats not covered by the on-road point counts. Each segment of 100 points will require up to 10 person-days during the same period as on-road counts, and assumes about 10 stations per day are covered along trails or cross-country.

Priority V. Additional Work—When resources are available, we recommend that the unit add programs, in increments of 10 person-days, of the three programs (II-IV) above. We do encourage additions of programs in the order they are recommended. However, local conditions, variety of habitat types, length of sampling season, areas of management concern, and consultation with biostatisticians will modify the order and magnitude of additional work in each unit. Additionally, at some point a unit will be best served collecting information other than that outlined above.

Selection of a Station Location

A monitoring station should be located in representative habitat for a given region, or in a habitat of concern. A station may have a variety of habitat types, and some will have a higher density of birds than others. Because the derived population and demographic parameters are likely to be highly sensitive to successional changes in the habitats sampled, stations should not be placed in very young habitats. However, young habitats are acceptable if they are held in a lower successional stage by active management.

If the census methods involve extensive point counts, the points can be spread out along a road or trail network, over a fairly large area of the region. This makes for a robust data set, because each point is at a location somewhat representative of the habitats in the region. In spot mapping and nest searches, a plot is usually established in a single habitat type, and is usually square or rectangular. Plots in heterogeneous habitat are often not as useful because they are more difficult to generalize about.

For constant-effort mist netting, we suggest the capture array be placed where a high rate of capture can be achieved. By contrast, extensive census points and the nest search plot should be placed in the representative habitats of the region.

Permanent Stations

While the need for broad-scale monitoring is of vital importance, in-depth studies in small, protected areas, such as natural areas, nature reserves, and parks, can contribute greatly to our knowledge of landbird populations. In-depth studies of bird life histories (normally using individually color-banded birds) can provide important insights into vulnerability and management of species. Other biological studies concurrently conducted at the station can add greatly to our knowledge of the factors affecting local landbird populations. Monitoring stations with active field programs or living quarters for biologists are ideal for intensive programs in remote areas and can often attract volunteers.

Obtaining institutional sponsorship of permanent stations can provide long-term commitment over many years. A monitoring program with such a commitment will continue despite turnover in personnel and can provide some stability in funding. Furthermore, by using local volunteers to collect data in such a program, a community outreach and education program can be established. Bird observatories and some university field stations in North and Latin America have been conducting programs similar to this for many years.

General Monitoring Procedures

Species To Be Covered

Although many species will be censused at a single station, fewer will be captured, and still fewer species will have their nests found. However, biologists at a single station should get a good sample of the population size of perhaps 30 species and

4

USDA Forest Service Gen. Tech. Rep. PSW-GTR-144-www. 1993.

some indication of demographics on about 10 species. In a region with perhaps six stations, more species will be monitored. Over a wide geographic area, these data can be combined to produce patterns of the population sizes and demographics of many species.

Monitoring Period
Breeding Season

The period of study for the breeding season differs, depending upon the individual species, latitude, rainfall pattern, temperature, elevation, or even year. Therefore, each region should establish its own monitoring period on the basis of the local breeding season and the criteria described below.

Demographic monitoring, by mist nets or nest searches, should span the entire breeding season. Censusing, by contrast, is usually conducted only during approximately the first half of the breeding season, when birds are most active, paired, on territories, and vocal.

For all monitoring, we recommend the use of the sampling interval time period of 10 days, as used in the British CES project, for several reasons. This interval allows at least one weekend for making up for inclement weather, and divides the month into three approximately equal portions. It also provides a basis for direct comparison between stations.

Operation of the demographic monitoring station by mist netting or nest searching should begin no sooner than the 10-day interval when virtually all of the breeding birds have established territories, but before many have begun laying eggs. For most lower elevation areas in temperate North America this will be about May 1 or May 11. The date, however, should be adjusted to conform with the local situation. For example, in the more northern parts of the United States, the first period can begin May 21 or May 31. In Alaska or northern Canada, or at high altitudes, the first period may begin as late as June 10. In the southwestern United States or coastal southern California, where 90 percent of the species have begun nesting activities by mid to late March, the starting date could be April 1 or 10. In Mexico, it could be even earlier, and in much of Latin America it could be much earlier. It is considered important by some investigators to avoid netting before migrant individuals of breeding species have finished moving through. Early netting might result in later net avoidance during the breeding season, thus biasing a few of the demographic estimates. However, some adjustment for this factor can be made during analysis and many stations do this with good results.

A good measure of the establishment of territories is increased singing. Also, captured males will show a pronounced cloacal protuberance. Individuals carrying nesting material is another excellent indication that the breeding season is under way. The best measure of the start of the breeding season is the beginning of egg laying. Females normally develop a brood patch when the first egg is laid.

The termination of the demographic monitoring should be no earlier than when the local population begins to be augmented by fall migrants, or by an increase of dispersing individuals known to have not bred in the local area. In most of temperate North America, this will usually be about the second or third 10-day interval of August.

For uniformity, May 1 of each year should be considered the first 10-day period. If a season in a region begins earlier, it should be backdated from May 1. In fact, the season of monitoring for most areas in temperate North America will begin May 1 and continue for a maximum of twelve 10-day intervals until August 28. If a station begins before May 1, it should continue until late August, unless a pilot project's data indicate that all breeding individuals and their young have left earlier.

For most of temperate North America, we recommend, therefore, the following periods: May 1-10, May 11-20, May 21-30, May 31-June 9, June 10-19, June 20-29, June 30-July 9, July 10-19, July 20-29, July 30-August 8, August 9-18, and August 19-28.

Censuses conducted on demographic study stations, such as mist netting stations, need be done only in the first five 10-day intervals when birds are on territory and actively singing. In temperate North America, this will be usually from May 1 through June 19. In northern latitudes or higher elevations, the period could be as late as June 1 to July 9. Point censuses, and also area searches, should be done once on each plot in each of the five 10-day intervals, and preferably about the mid-point of the interval.

Migration Operation

Operating a monitoring station in the spring or fall is an option in many areas. Spring and fall migration data from mist nets and censuses are confounded by many factors, particularly local weather, and the questions migration data can answer are different from those netting during the breeding season can answer. The data can provide interesting and insightful information about the timing, composition, and extent of migration (e.g., Ralph 1978, 1981a; Robbins and others 1959). The fall migration in particular gives a measure, derived from many source areas, of the overall productivity of a species. As mentioned previously, if a mist net program is operated in the spring in the same area as a breeding mist net array, a few demographic measures may be altered somewhat.

Nonbreeding Season

The value of winter studies is quite high. Winter is a time when populations are resident and relatively stable, thus providing excellent data on survivorship and mortality. It is very likely that habitat associations, for example, are much more defined in the winter than in the summer (e.g., Huff and others 1991, Manuwal and Huff 1987). The methods outlined here have full applicability in the non-breeding seasons, both in North America and Latin America. In the tropics, mist netting throughout the year at the same site would clarify many questions about molt, skull, and plumage patterns.

Maintenance of a Study Plot

Plots should be permanently marked with stakes, markers, or flagging that will survive over at least one winter. Rebar

USDA Forest Service Gen. Tech. Rep. PSW-GTR-144-www. 1993.

5

(steel reinforcing bar), rock cairns, or tags driven into landmarks all work well. Tags are available from biological supply companies. In general, markers should be laid out along a compass direction, be placed at regular intervals, and be visible at any point between the markers. Each marker should correspond to a numbered grid point on a map. In colder areas, be aware that in years with heavy snowfall, plot markers can still be buried in the spring. Net and census points should also be permanently marked. Be sure to record in your journal net height and angle of placement (use stakes or give a compass direction).

Customized maps of the study area should be traced from a large scale map or from aerial photographs. Landmarks, grid points, and net and census points should also be sketched. Blank maps can be used for spot mapping censuses, vegetation mapping, and other figures.

Each monitoring station ideally should be operated indefinitely. Although objectives will vary, we suggest that at a minimum, capture arrays of nets and nest searches should be operated for four consecutive years, and census plots for three years.

Journal Keeping

Journal keeping is an essential tool of all field biologists. The importance of regular, accurate journal keeping cannot be overemphasized. It is not uncommon for journals to be subpoenaed in court. The Grinnell method (Herman 1989) is the most widely used by vertebrate ecologists and is extremely detailed. Here we provide guidelines for basic information that may be useful for monitoring landbird populations.

As a minimum we recommend recording the following on a daily basis:
• Netting information: (a) the number and location of each net operated; (b) the exact hours of each net operated; and (c) the total capture and recapture rate for each species at each monitoring array.
• Censuses and nest searches: the number, location, and timing of each census conducted and the hours of nest searches.
• Personnel information: list the activities of each biologist conducting field work, including areas censused, net locations operated, and other activities.
• List of all birds seen or heard: basically presence/absence data; provide any interesting notes on potential breeding or other behavior of note.
• Weather data: in addition to the basic weather data that should be taken (see below), a general one- or two-sentence statement on the day's weather is also helpful.
• Plant phenology: a list of what is blooming or in seed may help interpret changes in bird distribution.
• Interesting observations of mammals, herptiles, insects, and other natural history observations should also be included.

Training and Numbers of Personnel

Training is extremely important because the level of training and experience will greatly affect the reliability of the data collected. Training *must* be something that is continuous throughout the field season. It is necessary to transmit expectations early and often in data taking or responsibilities for certain tasks.

The length of time to train personnel will vary greatly depending upon the quality and interest of recruits. For many census procedures, the mechanical aspects can be taught in two or three 2-hour sessions. However, for a person who has minimal skill in identification of plant or animal taxa, it can take a week or longer, depending upon the taxon, and the person's previous experience. The suggestions for censusers in Kepler and Scott (1981) are especially relevant. For a completely untrained person to learn to remove birds from mist nets takes at least 2-3 weeks of intensive training. This training should include at least 3-4 hours of removing birds from nets each day. Training for nest searching requires a similar time commitment.

Probably the most important aspect of training is the testing of the observer. This should be done regularly in the field by the most experienced personnel available to make sure that data are accurate, and of high quality. This can also be accomplished by regularly checking data sheets *as they come in from the field*. Any delay prevents feedback to the field crews.

The number of persons required to operate a monitoring station depends upon several factors. If nets are the method of choice, we suggest a minimum of two people, one of whom is well-trained in removing birds from mist nets, and one of whom is well-trained in identification of birds by sight, song, and call. The less skilled person can be of great assistance, and with proper training can contribute much to the monitoring. Censuses and netting are both morning activities, and under some circumstances they can be conducted concurrently if the censuser's position is known to the netter and he or she can be called upon for help if capture rate is moderately high. The health of the birds is of paramount importance, and all efforts to prevent injury must be taken. Nest searches can be conducted throughout the day, although it is most productive in the morning.

When conducting censuses, it is best to rotate observers, if at all possible, so that no observer censuses any given point more than the others.

Syllabi for training in the methods contained in this handbook have been prepared. These are for the use of persons experienced in the methods, so that they can efficiently pass on the methods to others. The syllabi are available from the senior author.

Data To Be Taken

Below we outline several types of data to be taken and provide sample forms for each. We have also prepared data entry programs using IBM compatible computers for these forms. Clean forms for reproduction and these programs can be obtained by contacting the senior author. These programs can use either standard entry systems such as dBASE or simple BASIC compilers.

For each point count census point, mist net location, and nest site, we suggest that the "Location and Vegetation Form" be filled out. It is described in detail in the Habitat Assessment section and contains important location information for data base files. At the minimum, for all monitoring programs, this location data should be taken.

All the data forms have constant the following information, to help relate between data bases:

• State or province—The 2-column code for each.

• Region—An 8-column code, designated by the investigator. Often, the name of the USGS quad, a prominent landmark, or a nearby town will provide the best code name.

• Station/Location—This is a 6-column unique identifier designated by the investigator to separate, within each region, the location of the various data points. We recommend that the station be a 4-letter code. The net location, point count census point, or nest number will be a 2-number code.

Constant-Effort Mist Nets and Banding

Scope

The capture of birds in nets can give the biologist an insight into the health and demographics of the population of the birds being studied. For instance, the proportion of young birds captured in mist nets has been shown to be a good measure of the productivity of birds during the previous few weeks (Baillie and others 1986). The sex ratio of a population can be used to assess the species' differential survivorship the previous year and the ability of the population to increase. The mist net capture rate gives a measure of the number surviving during the previous winter. The marking of individuals gives the biologist insight into degree of dispersal between different habitats and survivorship between years (e.g., Peach and others 1991). Finally, weight, when compared to measures of body size such as wing length, can give a measure of individual fitness.

Mist nets have been used for a long period to capture birds. Recently they have been used to monitor populations. Although some have used them to assay population size (e.g., Karr 1981), for most species, censuses are the best method for this, as netting provides relatively fewer data points per unit time. Netting, however, is the method of choice to provide information about the various attributes of the population, for instance, age and sex ratios and physiological condition.

Over the years numerous aids have been developed for field workers, with an emphasis on capture techniques and data taking (e.g., Baldwin 1931, Bub 1991, Lincoln 1947, Lincoln and Baldwin 1929, Lockley and Russell 1953, McClure 1984). O.L. Austin introduced mist nets to North American biologists in 1947 (Keyes and Grue 1982), and he, Low (1957), and Bleitz (1957) were all pioneers in their use.

The procedure detailed below is essentially identical to the "Constant Effort Sites" (CES) Scheme of the British Trust for Ornithology (Baillie and others 1986). The standards of operation are also identical to those of the Monitoring Avian Productivity and Survivorship Program (MAPS) (DeSante 1992a). We suggest the use of a series of mist net arrays, as in the British program, to be operated on 10 to 12 intervals during the breeding season, coupled with point count censuses. These data will provide an index of **adult population** size and changes at each station. The proportion of young birds in the catch will provide a measure of post-fledgling **productivity**. And finally, between-year recaptures can provide a sensitive measure of adult **survivorship** and **recruitment**. With these data, managers will have information on the possible causes of landbird declines or their remedies.

The monitoring of populations with mist nets is no more complicated than other techniques, but placement and operation should be done rather uniformly; thus we present below more details about this method than about others.

Net Placement

Operating a capture array of mist nets is a complex undertaking, but very rewarding. Much useful information can be gained from reading Bleitz (1970), Keyes and Grue (1982), or McClure (1984). We outline below some guidelines for operation of nets and their placement (*fig. 1*).

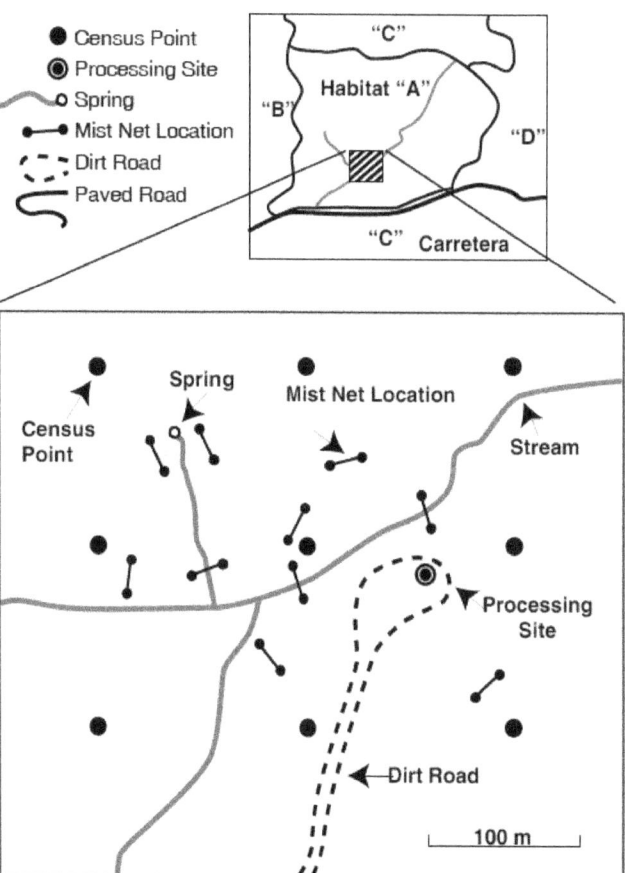

Figure 1—An idealized capture station of about 40 acres (16 ha) set in an area of more than 250 acres of habitat "A." Nine census points are set at uniform spacing of about 150 m to estimate population levels. Ten net locations are placed in sites where high capture rates are likely, along a stream, near a spring, and other areas where vegetation is dense, in order to monitor population and demographic parameters.

USDA Forest Service Gen. Tech. Rep. PSW-GTR-144-www. 1993.

7

A field crew of two people can usually set up and monitor an array of 8-12 mist nets quite easily. We suggest 10 as an appropriate number. If the biologists are especially skilled, or the bird density quite low, a few more nets may be operated. However, if too many nets are established in an array early in the season when capture rates are relatively low, the likely influx of post-breeding birds later in the season, in July and August, may severely tax the crew's resources.

Distance between nets is a very important consideration because of the effect of net dispersion on the precision of data from capture-recapture analyses. In order to increase the probability of capturing a bird banded the previous year, one should place the nets as far apart as possible, thus intersecting the most territories. However, it is absolutely critical that nets also be close enough to each other that a person can visit all net locations in a maximum of 10-15 minutes walking, preferably less, if no birds are caught. On flat, level terrain, this array would be about 0.5-0.6 miles (800-1000 m) in length. If 10 nets are placed in a circle or rectangle, this would allow about an average of 75-100 m between nets, and would cover approximately 5-10 ha. In steep or rough terrain, nets should be closer, and the area covered less. In all cases, nets should be spread out as uniformly as possible.

Nets should be placed at the same location and orientation for all 10-day intervals in each year and preferably between years. In the event the vegetation changes between years at a given location, the nets will measure this change, rather than changes in population of the birds. For this reason, care should be exercised in placing nets in locations where the vegetation will remain relatively stable through the life of the study. For example, successional changes, for instance, from a clear-cut to pole-sized trees over 10 years, would be unacceptable for a site. However, when the changes over a decade would be much less marked, the site would be permitted. If, due to unforeseen circumstances, the vegetation is changed markedly at one or two net locations of an array, the nets can be moved to locations with similar vegetation to allow better between-year comparisons. This should be a last resort, and only done after consultation with knowledgeable participants in the program.

Although few problems arise from placement of census points in areas of relatively high human impact, capture arrays must be located with more care. In some areas nets can be left in place (but closed) between capture days if the chance of encounter by visitors is extremely low. In most areas, it is advisable to rig the nets to allow easy removal at the close of a day's effort.

Baiting, artificial water, or taped vocalizations should not be used at any time to attract birds to the nets.

Net Locations

The best locations for the nets are usually on an edge of a habitat. Examples of edges include the boundary between a forest and a field, the boundary between two forests types (e.g., an upland pine and a pine/alder association in a valley), brushy portions of wooded areas, at the edge of a pond, and along a riparian corridor. Especially productive are areas where a habitat type has a narrow section, for instance a hedgerow, that narrows at a gate or where a natural gap funnels the vegetation along a watercourse. Birds, especially shrub species, will naturally be funneled into a net at that spot. Observations of bird movements will often suggest appropriate net locations.

The highest rate of capture is usually found in wetter areas within a given habitat type. If at all possible, natural running or pooled water should be available throughout the summer in the capture array, as it will draw birds from the immediate area. An array aside a major watercourse with a well-developed and wide riparian corridor will tend to monitor this habitat, but will also monitor the surrounding habitats. In many regions of the country, the riparian zone is the only place where sufficient numbers of birds can be captured.

The major goal of a mist net array is to capture birds, not to monitor the birds of a specific habitat. Census methods or nest search are more appropriate for this. An array set in a uniform habitat, such as an old-growth stand of coniferous trees, will usually catch relatively few birds, even if located along a watercourse in that habitat. There are possible exceptions to this, such as eastern deciduous forests (T. Sherry, pers. comm.).

A reasonable goal for capture rate is approximately two birds per net per day. This would result in the capture of approximately 200 or more birds during the season. Typically, the capture rate in the breeding season will be high during the first 10-day period, decline thereafter, and usually increase again during post-breeding dispersal, in July and August in temperate North America.

Erecting and Operating Nets

In order to operate nets properly, the trammels (the horizontal shelf strings that support the net) should be taut horizontally. Except with 6-m nets, this usually involves the use of tie cords bracing the pole upright. These can be arranged at 120° angles to the net, with one end secured to the pole and the other to nearby rocks, bushes, or stakes. When operated, the netting material should not be stretched apart to its full extent, but should allow some slack between the trammel lines; otherwise birds will bounce off the tight net.

If the habitat is higher than the typical net height of 2.5 or 3 meters above the ground, a stacked net can be considered. Although some birds may be missed, it is better to use single nets, rather than to stack them one above another, unless a particular location has a great abundance of birds. Even canopy-dwelling species invariably spend at least some time at lower levels, whether to nest, take water, or forage. The additional time spent putting up a stacked net can usually be better employed by establishing another net in the array. McClure (1984) describes several plans to stack nets; the simplest is to use a strong metal pole, perhaps 8-10 feet long, such as metal electrical conduit pipe. Connect two lengths together with a sleeve (a 10-cm section of conduit slipped over a 20-cm long pipe and glued in place), and tether the pole with a rope. The net can be easily lowered and raised using this method.

For single nets, we suggest the following simple method of putting them in place, adapted from Dennis P. Vroman (pers.

comm.). Clear all vegetation from a net lane 2 m wide to prevent vegetation from becoming entangled in the net. Drive one piece of 1-m by 3/8-inch piece of steel reinforcing bar (rebar) into the ground with a small hand sledge hammer at one end of the net lane on a slight backward angle to the net. Insert a 5-foot section of sawn 10-foot, 0.5-inch or larger, galvanized steel conduit over the rebar. Repeat at the other end of the net lane.

A single net can be kept on a round metal spool (used to hold bulk electrical wire), with a 6.5-inch diameter rim and 3.5- to 4-inch long axle or shaft. Place the loops of the net over the top of the upright conduit; then unroll the net towards the second pole, being careful to keep the loops in order. A second 5-foot section can be placed on each pole in a conduit connector or a sleeve atop the first conduit to allow the net to be fully opened.

When a net is to be closed, it should be spun to keep it from unraveling. To do this most effectively (preferably with two people from both ends simultaneously), leave the topmost trammel separated from the others on the pole, and spin the net on the lower trammels into a tight roll. Then quickly bring the top trammel down atop the roll to keep it from unraveling. This will allow the net to be opened much more quickly than if the net had been spun around all the trammel lines.

To roll up the net, keep all the support cords together and centered on the axle as the net is rolled up to allow easy unrolling. Use a rubber band to hold the loops in place at the end of the rolled net. Poles and rebar can be hidden under vegetation near the net location to save set-up time.

Nets are also commonly put in cloth bags. To take down the net, it is rolled up on small folds and put into the bag, as the biologist moves from one end towards the other.

Net Specifications and Maintenance

A variety of net types can be purchased, but we strongly suggest that the same type be used throughout the life of the study. The net color should be black in forest or brush habitats. The net mesh should be either 30 mm or 36 mm in stretched diameter. The larger net catches more thrush-sized birds, but smaller birds can become more severely tangled. Nets 12 m in length are preferred, although in certain sites a half-net of 6 m long can prove useful. (If a 6-m net is used, its use for one hour equals a half net-hour.) In addition, some suppliers offer "extra-full" nets that provide more capture area. They also offer "tethered" nets that are resistant to bunching by the wind because they are fastened to the trammels. If a nontethered net is obtained, it can easily be tethered by placing drops of a liquid cement along the top trammel.

A net should be replaced when it fades badly or becomes degraded by the sun so that it breaks very readily. A net can be tested by putting two fingers into the net and gently parting them. Nets sustain damage from branches, misuse, large birds, and from the rare occasions when a badly tangled bird must be cut out of the netting. The life can be prolonged by repairs with a strong black nylon twine or thread. Holes should be repaired promptly, or the net replaced, as they affect the efficiency of capture, and make it difficult to figure out how to extract a bird.

Operation of Nets

Net Hours

To minimize variability and make comparisons from different locations, standardization of the number of nets and the number of hours nets are operated has long been advocated. It is extremely important that nets be operated on the same schedule between years, so as to allow direct comparisons. A standard "net" is considered to be 12 m long and 2.5 m high. For calculating effort, one standard mist net operated for one hour is a "net-hour." Two nets stacked atop one another would be considered two nets, although one net location. If operated for one hour, they would total two net-hours.

Although there are methods of compensating for varying number of nets operated in different time periods (Ralph 1976), these are best implemented during migratory periods when there is a high turnover of individuals between days. During the breeding season, when populations are more stable, it is best to operate nets on as regular a schedule as possible. This includes the number of nets, the number of hours, the time of day, the number of days, and the number of days between operations.

We recommend that biologists use the "Record of Net-Hours" form *(fig. 2)*. The data are recorded on a daily basis, as follows:
 • State or province—The 2-column code for each.
 • Region—An 8-column code, designated by the investigator. Often, the name of the USGS quad, a prominent landmark, or a nearby town will provide the best code name.
 • Station—A 4-letter code for the station that contains the mist net array.
 • Year.
 • Operator(s).
 • Net location—Place a 2-column number identifying each net location. Most arrays will have no more than 10 locations, and thus would be numbered 1-10.
 • Number of nets—This number is usually one, but if a stacked net is used, or if a net is within 10 m of another, they are considered the same location, and the number of nets is entered here.
 • Month and day—One line for each day of operation, but if a net location is operated for more or less time than the other nets, it should get a line to itself.
 • Open and close times—Using the 24-hour clock, record the time of starting to open and the time of starting to close the nets.
 • Hours open—Calculate the number of hours open to the nearest tenth of an hour (e.g., 4 hours, 20 minutes is 4.3 hours).
 • Number of net-hours—Multiply the number of nets by the hours open, and enter here.
 • Total net-hours—For each day, total the number of net-hours.

Time of Day and Number of Checks

Nets should be opened within 15 minutes of local sunrise and operated for a minimum of 4, and preferably 6, hours per

RECORD OF NET-HOURS

STATE `C A` REGION `MT SHASTA` STATION `BEVA` YEAR `1992` OPERATOR(S): Jane Birder, Bill Bass

NET LOCATION:	1	2	3	4	5	6	7	8	9	10						TOTAL NETS
NUMBER OF NETS:	1	1	2	1	1	1	3	1	1	1						13

MO./DAY	OPEN TIME	CLOSE TIME	HOURS OPEN	NUMBER OF NET-HOURS PER LOCATION																TOTAL NET-HOURS
6/6	0530	1030	5.0	5.0	5.0	10.0	5.0	5.0	5.0	15.0	5.0	5.0	5.0							65.0
6/7	0535	1035	5.0	5.0	5.0	10.0	5.0	5.0	5.0	15.0	5.0	5.0	5.0							65.0
6/8	0530	1050	5.3	5.3	5.3	10.6	5.3	5.3	5.3	15.9	5.3	5.3	5.3							67.9
6/9	0530	1030	5.0	5.0	5.0	10.0	—	5.0	5.0	15.0	5.0	5.0	5.0							60.0
6/9	0830	1030	2.0	—	—	—	2.0	—	—	—	—	—	—							2.0
6/10	0540	1040	5.0	5.0	5.0	10.0	5.0	5.0	5.0	15.0	5.0	5.0	5.0							65.0

Figure 2—The "Record of Net-Hours," for recording and summarizing net-hours.

day. Nets should be checked every 45 minutes (more often in inclement or very hot weather) and absolutely not more than once each hour. That is, the net round should begin no longer than 45 minutes after the *start* of the previous round. Nets should be opened in the same order each day, and closed in the same order that they were opened. It is very desirable that the number of hours for each net location should be the same for all 10-day intervals and for all years. Each station should be operated once per 10-day monitoring interval throughout the breeding season. We recommend that arrays be run no more than once per 10-day interval. Running arrays more than twice per interval greatly lowers capture probability per net hour. If sufficient time is available, it is far more productive to set up another array, rather than increasing effort at a single station.

When To Close Nets

The nets should not be operated in rain, wind, and extreme heat. If already open when these conditions occur, they should be closed, because precipitation is heavy enough for the birds' feathers to become wet enough to lose their insulation. Strong winds can cause severe tangling. In general, a steady wind of more than 10 mph or occasional gusts to more than 15 mph should be watched carefully for their effect on netted birds, and the nets should be closed if necessary. Finally, in situations with excessive heat and direct sunlight with little wind, netted birds can quickly overheat and die. On such hot days, birds should not remain in an exposed net for more than 15 minutes.

A certain amount of mortality may occur whenever wildlife is handled or trapped. However, mortality rates in most netting projects usually approach zero, and generally average less than 1 percent when mortality does occur. If mortality consistently occurs in nets, or exceeds an average of 1 percent, it is likely that birds are not being processed quickly enough, probably during their removal from the nets. Under these circumstances, scrutinize closely the criteria for closing nets and the expertise of the people running the station.

Removing Birds from Nets

Below we suggest some methods for extracting birds from mist nets. The methods are used by most netters, were derived

10

USDA Forest Service Gen. Tech. Rep. PSW-GTR-144-www. 1993.

from ideas of Shreve (1965), and were later modified and augmented by Ralph (1967, 1988). Practice and careful review of these techniques are essential. Most importantly, be careful. The life and health of the birds are of primary concern.

As you work on a badly tangled bird, it is important to remember that the bird can usually be backed out easily, unharmed, in the direction from which it entered the net. You *must first* take the time necessary to figure out exactly how the bird went into the net. Observe carefully from which side the bird entered the net, and between which trammels it went, in order to find the opening of the pocket the bird made. Do not just grab the bird, tempting as it may be. Start on the side of the net which the bird entered; part the trammels and netting loosely, and look into the pocket caused by the weight of the bird. Because the tail is the last to enter, look at its position to get a clue about how the bird entered the net. Back the bird out the way it went in, step by step. A light touch is the most important prerequisite for all methods. After determining where the bird entered, several standard procedures are used for removing birds, but different species and different problems will require some improvisation.

We describe the various methods used to remove birds from nets below. No one method will suffice for all birds, because each bird flies into a net differently. Combinations of methods will often be necessary. In all methods it is often desirable to know where the strands of net are amongst the bird's feathers. This knowledge can help you decide where to move your fingers next. By far the best method is to pull gently at the exposed netting and see where feathers move on the bird. This will tell you where the net strands are binding, leading to quicker removal.

Body Grasp Method

This method has recently been used by some stations, and it has been found to surpass other methods in ease of learning, reduced injury to the birds, and speed of removal. About 9 of 10 birds can be removed with this method.

1. Find out from which side of the net the bird entered. Find the opening of the pocket caused by the weight of the bird.

2. You have three choices at this point. (1) If the bird's body is accessible, without any netting in the way, and the net free of the back and head, just put the bird into the "bander's grip," with your palm against its back, your index and middle fingers on either side of the neck, the left wing held with your thumb, and the other fingers curled around the body and the right wing. Then proceed to step #7 below. (2) If the net is tangled around the head and wing, just slip your fingers over the body and under the wings. This usually involves your thumb around the breast and your fingers over the bird's back, and down over its sides and under the wings and carefully around the curve of the body. (3) If the body is too tangled to be available for a body grasp, then one of the other methods below must be used.

3. With the body now firmly secured, back the body out of the net to expose at least the bend of one of the wings. Then, remove the net from the wings. Flick net threads from the bend of the wings, working from the underside. Generally your thumb should be placed under the thread(s) on the underside of the wing and your forefinger placed on the outer bend of the wing as a fulcrum to flick the thread over. Often at this stage it is helpful to pull gently on the exposed portions of the still tangled threads in order to free them or to see where they are caught.

4. When one wing is free, slip your fingers over the now-exposed wing, securing it against the bird's body. Then, pull remaining loops from around the neck, working from the back of the head forward, in the manner of removing a T-shirt.

5. Remove the net from the other wing, as above.

6. The bird should now have gradually been put into the "bander's grip."

7. Pull the bird up and away from the net, and it will usually free its own feet in an effort to fly. If the toes are caught, untangle them by pulling strands gently. You will notice that if the heel joint is straightened out, the bird's toes have a tendency to relax, so that the netting can be more easily removed. If the bird is clutching the net firmly, extract the feet by (1) first freeing the opposable toe (the "thumb") by sliding the threads over it and lifting it away from the other toes; (2) with the fingers, straightening the other three toes out; and (3) sliding the netting over the toes with repeated strokes.

This method, when administered with a nimble hand and a light touch, is very easy on the bird because the only firm contact is on the sides of the neck. It is also a time saver, because feet untangle themselves. The method works best with a recently caught bird that has had little time to entangle itself, but is applicable to most birds.

Feet First Method

The original, and perhaps still the most widely used method, is somewhat slower but is usually the way that beginners are taught. Its main disadvantage is that it requires holding the legs, sometimes causing injury or breakage. It involves the following steps:

1. As before, find the side of the net the bird entered.

2. If you (the bander) are right-handed, grasp both tibiae (the tibia is the feathered part of the leg above the bare tarsus) from the rear of the bird using your left hand so that your fingers point towards the bird's head. The bird should be upside down in the net when you have your grip.

3. Put your index finger between the tibiae, and press your thumb against the bird's right tibia and your middle finger against the left tibia. This leaves your right hand free to remove net strands from the entangled legs and feet.

4. Most importantly, make certain that all threads are pulled down and off tibiae and thighs below the heel joint, the prominent joint between the tibia and tarsus. These threads are sometimes high up on the thigh at the flank.

5. Untangle the toes by the method described in the body grasp method above.

6. Pull the bird up and away from the net, still holding the bird upside down by the feathered tibiae, above the bare tarsus. Flick net threads from the bend of the wings, working from the underside. Generally the thumb should be placed

under the thread(s) on the underside of the wing and the forefinger placed on the outer bend of the wing as a fulcrum to flick the thread over. Often at this stage it is helpful to pull gently on the exposed portions of the still tangled threads in order to free them or to see where they are caught.

7. When both wings are free, pull remaining loops from around the neck, working from the back of the head forward. Be sure to secure the bill by placing the thumb against the tip while pulling the net over the head in order to protect the delicate neck.

Rollover Method

A third method requires a little practice but is applicable to almost every situation:

1. As always, determine the side of the net entered.

2. Grasp the left (or right) leg above the tarsus and release the foot.

3. Release the left (or right) wing; release the head, then the other wing. Grasp the bird normally with the "bander's grip." Finally, free the right foot.

This method requires an experienced "feel"—the bird is rolled over and released in order of foot, wing, head, wing, and foot. This method is especially recommended when one of the legs is particularly badly tangled. Work so as to free that leg last.

Processing

Once the birds are removed from the nets, put each individual in a separate, small cloth bag, and transport to the processing site. It is probably best to have a central processing site, rather than to process birds at each net as they are captured, because: (1) a biologist rapidly circulating around the nets can better monitor the captures, in case of an influx of birds that might necessitate shutting down some nets temporarily; and (2) it lessens the disturbance in the vicinity of the nets. Further, if processing becomes delayed, it is always preferred to have the birds out of the nets and stored in bags. Bags should be made from opaque cloth, and sewn so that the seams (and possible loose threads that can catch toes) are outside. Hang bags from hooks or branches to prevent them from being stepped on, and out of direct sunlight. They should be washed often.

Birds should be released at the processing site except for females (indicated by a brood patch) and dependent juveniles (indicated by a frizzy appearance and a growing tail). They should be released at the point of capture.

Recaptures provide the most important data in a constant-effort mist netting program. We suggest, if some birds have to be released without processing, that recaptures have a much higher priority for processing than unbanded birds. If birds have to be released without complete processing, we suggest that the following be regarded as the priorities, in order: (1) band number (if a recapture); (2) species; (3) age (usually involves skulling, or diagnostic plumage characters); (4) new band number (if previously unbanded); (5) sex; and (6) other measurements or data. Please notice that the species and age are the two variables which are considered absolutely critical. If these are not accurately and completely recorded, the time and money spent in the monitoring has minimal value to the objectives.

Special Problems
Tongue Caught in Net

The mouth structure of birds, especially thrushes, thrashers, and woodpeckers, allows net threads to catch behind the tongue. While the bird's head is held between your index and middle finger, your third and fourth fingers and thumb can hold the net near the side of the mouth and relieve pressure on the tongue by pulling the net backward along the side of the head. A pencil, crochet hook, or a sharp twig can be manipulated with your free hand to lift the thread from behind the cleft of the tongue. Until one becomes deft at releasing the tongue in this manner, a small pair of a scissors is invaluable. Usually, clipping a single strand of mesh will do the trick.

Badly Caught Birds

As a last recourse, to remove a strand from a tongue, or to rapidly extract a bird in distress it is sometimes necessary to cut a few threads with a scissors, a stitch ripper (sewing tool that cuts threads along seams), or a sharp knife. The most rapid method is to find an area with few (or only one if possible) layers of netting. Clip as few strands as possible, just enough to bring the bird through the net. Then free the bird in the normal manner. It should be very rare to need to cut more than three strands. Before releasing such a bird, look carefully to ensure that no net remains on the bird.

Data Collection

One of the first steps a biologist must take to make the capture work more meaningful is to properly record the data presented each time that a bird is caught. Much of the following was extracted from Pyle and others (1987) and Ralph (1967, 1988). The identification guide by Pyle and others (1987) should be included in all netting kits.

At each net location, we suggest that the Location and Vegetation Form (fig. 15, discussed in detail below) be filled out. The Location information on the first three lines of the form is vital to data base management.

For each individual captured or recaptured, we recommend that the following data be recorded. In addition to date, time, and location, it is imperative that the species be accurately identified. It is also vital that the age and the sex of the birds be determined. We highly recommend that determining the amount of skull pneumatization be a top priority, as essentially all analyses depend upon accurate ageing. Age and sex determinations are generally complicated by the highly variable nature of size, plumage, and molt patterns in each species. We recognize that a certain percentage of individuals cannot be reliably aged, sexed, or identified with any one or even all of the published criteria. Remember that with age and sex it is better to be cautious than inaccurate. If the bander is unsure of an age/sex class, we recommend that the record be conservative, by recording the age or sex as unknown, and separately noting which class seems likely. By using the skull pneumatization and the literature carefully, determinations can be made with above 99 percent confidence. Information on how the bander aged and sexed the bird can be used to screen improperly processed birds. We also highly recommend that the breeding condition of adults, the extent of juvenal plumage and molt, and the wing chord also be recorded.

For the various attributes below we suggest a letter or numeric code. We strongly suggest that whatever codes are used at a station should be used consistently between years, or certainly within a year. Alpha (letter) codes have the advantage of being mnemonic in nature, increasing accuracy. Numeric codes have the advantage of retaining the order of progression from small, none, or few, to large or many.

Plumage Attributes

The first plumage (subsequent to the natal down) acquired by the nestling and retained by the juvenile fledgling is called the juvenal plumage (note the difference in spellings). The body feathers of this plumage are replaced during the first prebasic molt, which almost always occurs within three months of fledging and usually takes place on the breeding grounds. Juveniles are readily aged by many criteria and are generally sexually indistinguishable by plumage. The juvenal plumage is usually more streaked or spotted than that of the adult, and juveniles will often have wing bars where the adult has none. Juvenal feathers also have a more loosely structured contour *(fig. 3)*, most evident in the feathers of the nape, back, and undertail coverts. In addition, many nestling characteristics are evident in young juveniles which can also be helpful in separating them from adults. The gape of nestlings and early juveniles is swollen and more brightly colored than that in adults, and the inside of the mouth is also brighter in tone, or paler in hue, or both, in juveniles than in adults. Several characters useful for separating first-year birds from adults can be applied to juveniles. In particular, summer adults in alternate (breeding) plumage should show very worn flight feathers while those of juveniles should be relatively much fresher. And, of course, the pneumatization process is just beginning in juveniles, whereas it should be complete (or nearly so) in adults. Finally, eye color is useful for separating juveniles of many species, being generally grayer and paler in juveniles and redder and darker in adults. In summary, biologists

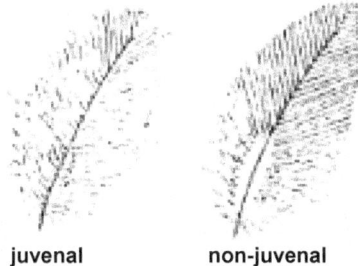

juvenal   **non-juvenal**

Figure 3—The contrast between juvenal and nonjuvenal body feathers. The differences are most apparent with undertail coverts and feathers of the nape and back. Taken from Pyle and others (1987).

should have no trouble with the separation of juveniles from adults during the summer months, when all criteria are used.

In most passerine species, however, birds in juvenal plumage cannot be reliably sexed by in-hand criteria alone. Only in a few species, in which differences occur in the color pattern of the flight feathers, can juveniles be sexed by plumage.

As juvenile birds go through their first molt, normally in the fall, they assume a plumage that is often similar to that of adults, especially to that of the adult female in sexually dimorphic (having a male and female plumage) species. Inspecting the skull is now recognized as being the most reliable technique for ageing these birds.

Age Classes

The various age codes suggested below follow, for the most part, the system used by the U.S. Fish and Wildlife Bird Banding Laboratory and the Canadian Wildlife Service Bird Banding Office, as listed in the North American Bird Banding Manual (CWS and USFWS 1991). The system is based primarily on the calendar year. Following are the age designation, the alpha code used by the Services, a suggested one-letter abbreviation (or optional numeric code) for purposes of this handbook (where different from the Services' code), and a definition of the age class.

Unknown (**U** or 0). Age cannot be determined with absolute confidence.

Local (**L** or 4). A young bird incapable of sustained flight.

Hatching Year (HY) (**H** or 2). A bird in its juvenal or first basic plumage during its first calendar year (i.e., from its fledging until December 31 of the year that it fledged).

Second Year (SY) (**S** or 5). A bird in its second calendar year (i.e., January 1 of the year following fledging through December 31 of the same year).

After Hatching Year (AHY) (**A** or 1). A bird in *at least* its second calendar year. This code is more significant after the breeding season, when it implies an adult. Before the breeding season, it essentially means "unknown" (either SY or ASY).

After Second Year (ASY or 6) (**O** [older]). An adult in at least its third calendar year (i.e., a bird in at least the year following its first breeding season and second prebasic molt). A bird known to be in its third year, or older, should be indicated by "O," and a note should be made in the Notes columns.

Skull Pneumatization

Determining the amount of skull pneumatization, also known as ossification, is the best method of ageing most species of birds during the summer and fall months and, for some species, is proving useful through the early winter and even into spring. The importance of this method cannot be understated. If you take only one datum besides species, skull pneumatization is quite probably the next most important.

This technique came into common usage in the late 1960's. Biologists are strongly urged to become proficient at skulling and to skull most passerine species throughout the year. When a fledgling passerine leaves the nest, the section of the skull overlaying the brain (frontals and parietal) consists of a single layer of bone. From fledging until the bird is four to 12 months old (depending mostly on the species), a second layer of bone develops underneath the first. The two layers are then separated slightly by spaces or air pockets and joined by small columns of bone. This process is called skull pneumatization.

The pattern generally follows one of the two progressions illustrated in *figure 4*, but may show other variations. Smaller species tend to show the peripheral pneumatization pattern, and larger species the median line pattern. Individuals of certain species may show either pattern, however, and the exact shapes of the unpneumatized areas or "windows" will also show substantial individual variation.

Any passerine found with a partially pneumatized skull *(fig. 4a-c)* can be reliably aged as a hatching year bird, with the exception perhaps of occasional summer or early fall birds with small windows *(fig. 4d)*. In most North American passerine species, the skulls of the earliest hatching year birds become completely pneumatized in October and November, and the latest birds become complete between November and January, but for purposes of this monitoring effort during the breeding season, all hatching year birds will have incomplete pneumatization.

In some (perhaps many) species, small unpneumatized windows may normally be retained until spring and even early summer. This is most commonly seen in the longer distance migrants such as certain flycatchers, swallows, thrushes, and vireos. Birds with windows greater than one millimeter in diameter *(fig. 4d)* are probably reliably aged as Second-years through June of their second year. Birds with smaller windows are not necessarily in their hatching year, because some small proportion (probably less than 1 percent) of individuals will never show complete pneumatization. Birds with small windows in July and August are most likely to be advanced young of that year.

The Process of Determining the Extent of Skull Pneumatization

Unpneumatized areas of the passerine skull usually appear pinkish or dull reddish, whereas pneumatized areas appear grayish, whitish, or pinkish-white, with small white dots indicating the columns of bone. The color or contrast between these two color patterns, or both, can usually be seen through the skin of the head, especially after the head has been wetted to allow parting of the feathers, and to make the skin more transparent.

To skull a passerine, start by holding the bird in the position shown in *figure 5*. This hold facilitates skulling because the skin can more readily be moved around the skull, allowing a large area of the skull to be viewed through a small area of skin. In order to see the skull, the feathers need to be parted such that a small opening of bare skin is created. This can be accomplished without wetting the feathers, but is much more easily done if a small amount of water is applied to the head (do not apply detergent or alcohol solutions). During cold weather, the few drops of water used to make the skin more transparent should have no effect on the bird's ability to

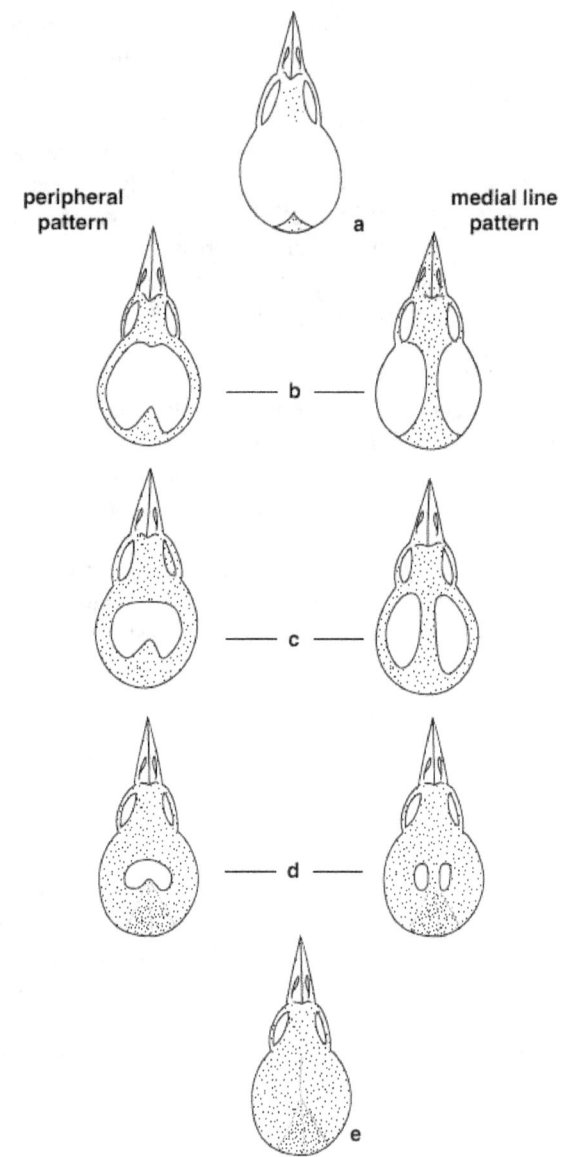

Figure 4—The two common patterns of skull pneumatization, from a very young bird ("a"), to a completely pneumatized bird ("e"). Taken from Pyle and others (1987).

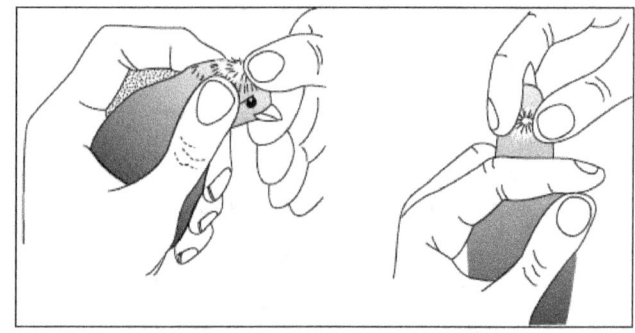

Figure 5—Two good holds for skulling a bird. It is best to look to the side of the mid-line of the skull. Taken from Pyle and others (1987).

14

USDA Forest Service Gen. Tech. Rep. PSW-GTR-144-www. 1993.

maintain its temperature. If there is concern about this, simply put the bird out of the wind in a dry bag for a few minutes before releasing it.

It is usually easiest to part the feathers by running your thumb or finger forward over the crown, against the direction in which the feathers lie, and then moving the feathers off to each side. In the summer and early fall, when most young birds are just beginning the pneumatization process, it is good to start at the rear and the side of the skull and work up towards the crown. Later in the fall, the parting should be made higher up on the crown (in the areas just above and behind the eyes), where the last unpneumatized windows usually occur. With thicker-skinned birds, one can improve viewing by parting the feathers on the side of the head or neck (where the skin is more transparent) and moving the skin up to the crown. When the skulling process is finished, the feathers can be smoothed back into place.

It is usually best to hold the bird under a fairly strong lamp or in indirect sunshine to achieve the best lighting conditions for viewing. Very bright light often creates a glare off the skin. It is often helpful to move the head around, because different angles of light can make it easier to see through the skin. We strongly recommend using a magnifying device such as a visor that slips over your head.

Move the skin back and forth—the spots will be stationary, and thus visible. *If the tiny white dots are not visible, one is not properly viewing the skull*, or the bird is a very young juvenile with an entirely pinkish skull. "Seeing" a boundary between whitish and pink areas is not enough, because one might be seeing only bone structure unrelated to pneumatization. Start looking at the skull at a point at its base and slightly to one side. Continue looking forward until just halfway between the eye and the top of the crown. If at no point the dots disappear and are replaced by a clear pink area, the skull is fully pneumatized. Because the pneumatization usually proceeds centripetally and anteriorly, be sure to examine the area between the eyes of all birds with pneumatized skulls, to make sure that they are not "advanced" immatures.

Also look for entirely pinkish skulls in very young birds *(fig. 4a)* in June-July and for contrasts between the pneumatized and unpneumatized areas in older birds (most frequently after August). Small windows *(fig. 4d)* should be carefully looked for at all times.

Any of several factors may make it difficult or impossible to see the pneumatization of the skull. These include: the skin of the head being too thick; large amounts of fat in the skin during fall migration and winter; and dark, or otherwise opaque, skin (especially in molting or injured birds). It is especially difficult to see the pneumatization of the skull in molting birds, because of the thickening and the excessive flaking of the skin.

We suggest codes for categories of skull pneumatization. Because the critical differences are often in the 0-5 percent or 95-100 percent categories, care should be taken. It can make a great deal of difference in evaluating the age during the breeding season to know that a skull had only small windows (e.g., 98 percent pneumatized) and could have been either a second-year bird or perhaps a young bird, as opposed to one that was perhaps 70 percent and almost assuredly a young bird.

The codes we suggest are:

N or 0 - **N**o white spots showing, only a single, thin layer of bone covers the entire brain.

T or 1 - **T**race of pneumatization at the very back of the skull, usually appearing as an opaque, grayish crescent or a very small triangular area. Between 1 and 5 percent of the skull is pneumatized.

L or 2 - **L**ess than one-third pneumatized, but some is obvious. Generally the posterior part of the cranium has a triangular or circular area of small white dots, usually distinctly contrasting with the nonpneumatized area.

H or 3 - **H**alf the skull pneumatized, between one-third and two-thirds complete. Typically, most of the rear half is complete, as well as part of the front, extending back to the eyes. The front is usually difficult to see, because of dense, short feathers.

G or 4 - **G**reater than two-thirds pneumatized, but at least a small area not complete, less than 95 percent complete.

A or 5 - **A**lmost complete pneumatization, between 95 percent and 99 percent complete. These birds show a tiny dull, pinkish area or "windows."

F or 6 - **F**ully complete pneumatization.

U - **U**nknown, skull examined, but extent of pneumatization not determinable.

Sex Determination

The best method for determining the sex of sexually monomorphic passerine birds during the breeding season is by the presence or absence of the cloacal protuberance in the male, and the brood patch, which primarily occurs in females. All North American landbirds develop at least one of these characteristics, at least partially, and most are reliably sexed by them during the late spring and summer months. Latin American birds are less well-known, but these guidelines should generally apply.

Cloacal Protuberance—In order to store sperm and to assist with copulation, external cloacal protuberances, or bulbs, are developed by male passerine birds during the breeding season. They usually begin to develop early in the spring and reach their peak size in 3-5 weeks. Depending on the species and the number of clutches attempted during the breeding season, cloacal protuberances will recede from mid to late summer.

Although the cloacal regions in females will sometimes swell slightly, or show a small protuberance, it rarely approaches the size of those in the males (the Wrentit appears to be an exception). If the swelling forms a gradual slope on the abdomen ending with the cloacal opening pointing towards the tail, then it is probably a female in breeding condition. When the female is most swollen in this area, she will usually also have a brood patch. A typical male protuberance essentially forms a right angle to the abdomen and is somewhat larger at the top than at the bottom.

USDA Forest Service Gen. Tech. Rep. PSW-GTR-144-www. 1993.

15

To view the protuberance, blow the feathers apart in the region of the vent. The shape of the protuberance can be somewhat variable, and nonbreeding males may not always develop one. After a little experience with the shape of the cloacal region during the nesting season, biologists should have no problem separating breeding males from females.

We have categorized cloacal protuberances into four size categories *(fig. 6)*: none (**N** or 0), small (**S** or 1), medium (**M** or 2), and large (**L** or 3). As one becomes familiar with the various extents of protuberances, one can make a judgment on the relative size.

Brood Patch—Incubation or brood patches are developed by incubating birds as a means of transferring as much body heat as possible to eggs or young in the nest. In most landbirds, females perform all or most of the incubating, and develop more substantial brood patches. The presence of a distinct brood patch can thus be used to reliably sex breeding females of almost all passerine species.

The development of the brood patch begins with the loss of the feathers of the abdomen, about 3-5 days before the first eggs are laid (Blake 1963). Shortly thereafter, the blood vessels of the region begin to increase in size, and the skin becomes thicker and filled with an opaque, whitish fluid. *Figure 7a* illustrates a full brood patch as viewed by blowing

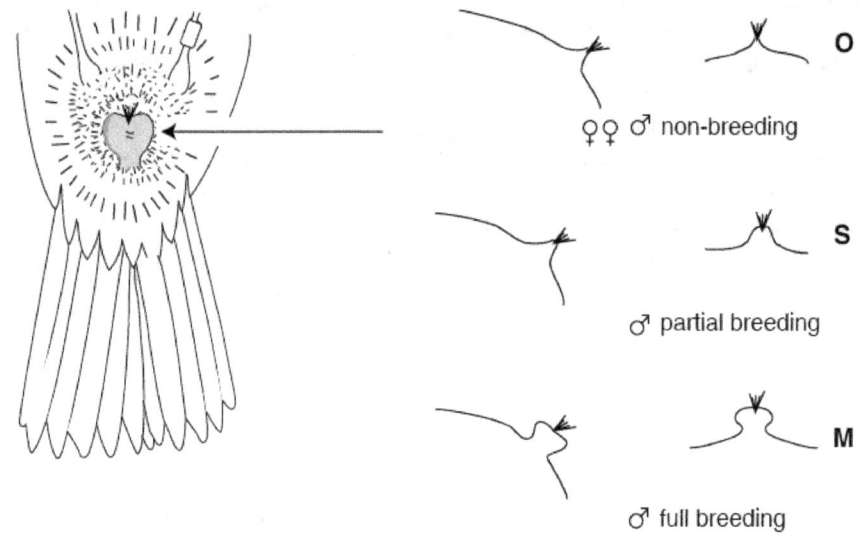

Figure 6—On the left, a cloacal protuberance at its peak in a male passerine. On the right a nonbreeding male (class = 0), a male beginning to be in breeding condition (class = S), and a male in full breeding condition (class = M). Class "L" would show a more prominent protuberance. Taken from Pyle and others (1987).

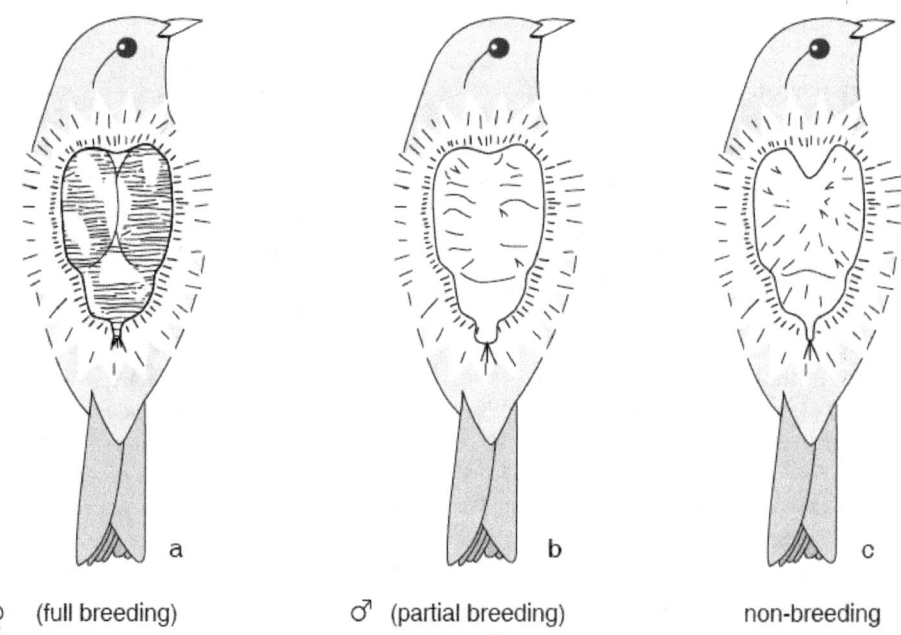

♀ (full breeding)   ♂ (partial breeding)   non-breeding

Figure 7—Brood patches in different stages of development. Taken from Pyle and others (1987).

USDA Forest Service Gen. Tech. Rep. PSW-GTR-144-www. 1993.

the feathers of the breast aside. A few days after the fledglings leave the nest, the swelling and blood vascularization will begin to subside. If a second clutch of eggs is laid, the process (except for defeathering) will be repeated. A new set of feathers on the abdomen are usually not grown until the prebasic molt, after completion of breeding. Between the end of nesting and the onset of molt, the skin of the abdomen will often appear grayish and wrinkled. Many young, and especially juvenile, passerine birds have little or no down or feathers on the belly; therefore the belly of some young look much like that of an adult who is just beginning to develop a brood patch, but the area will be quite smooth and usually a pink or dark red.

In most North American passerine birds, the male does not develop a brood patch in the breeding season. Slightly fewer feathers may be present on the abdomen than are found in the winter, but the breast retains a feathered appearance. In a few groups, in North America, notably the mimids, vireos, *Myiarchis* flycatchers, and a few other species (see Pyle and others 1987), the male will assist with incubation and develop an incomplete brood patch. This will include partial or complete feather loss and slight to moderate vascularization and swelling, which rarely or never approaches the extent of development typically found in females of the same species. Only in the Wrentit and the woodpeckers does the male develop a full brood patch.

We suggest recording brood patch in the order of its development as follows:

N or 0 - **N**o brood patch present—Breast more or less feathered. Nonfeathered areas of the breast and abdomen smooth without evident vascularization. In some species such as hummingbirds, and in most young birds, the breast is normally not feathered.

S or 1 - **S**mooth skin—A loss of breast and some abdomen feathers, but most of the area is still rather smooth and dark red.

V or 2 - **V**ascularized—Abdominal skin thickened with increased fluid and vascularization. This is the peak of incubation.

W or 3 - **W**rinkled—Abdomen skin thinning, wrinkly, and scaly.

M or 4 - **M**olting—New pin feathers are coming in on the abdomen. Nesting is usually completely over by this point.

Measurements

The standard reference for measuring birds is Baldwin and others (1931), which outlines virtually every possible measurement. Although old, it is commonly listed as available in catalogs of used natural history books.

Size, as indicated by specific measurements such as wing, tail, or tarsus length, is often a useful characteristic for identifying, ageing, and especially, for sexing passerine birds in the hand. In almost all passerine species, the size of males of a given population will average larger than that of the females by about 5-10 percent. The extent to which the sexes overlap in size depends on both the species and the particular measurement being considered. Measurements also vary with age, but to a lesser extent than with sex. For example, juvenal primaries tend to be slightly (2-5 percent) shorter than adult primaries. Within each sex class, immature birds with juvenal primaries will have shorter wing lengths than adults. When coupled with weight and fat, size can also give a strong indication of the health of a bird.

When identifying, ageing, or sexing passerine birds it is important to use measuring techniques that are strictly standardized with those of published samples. In the following sections we recommend standardized methods for obtaining the measurements. All linear measurements should be recorded in millimeters (mm).

Wing Length—Although various methods of measuring wings are employed, we recommend that you measure the wing chord, because this is the length most frequently used and most widely published for North American birds, and is the most consistent between measurements. The wing chord is measured from the bend of the wing to the tip of the longest primary, across the natural arc of the primaries *(fig. 8)*. While taking the wing measurement, avoid the tendency to flatten the natural curve of the wing, thus getting a measurement that is 2-5 percent longer than proper.

To measure the wing chord it is best to have a thin ruler with a perpendicular stop at zero. Insert the ruler under the wing, and place the bend of the wing (carpal joint or "wrist") snugly against the stop. To avoid differences due to carpal compression, we recommend that the bend of the wing be pushed against the stop with no more pressure than the wing itself applies when the ruler is moved up to the wing. Once the wing is in place, make sure that the line between the carpal joint and the tip of the longest primary is parallel with the edge of the ruler, gently lower its tip to the ruler so that it touches it, and read the wing chord length *(fig. 8)*.

When measuring the wing it is important to make sure that the longest primary is not broken, bent, or molting. Bent primary tips should be straightened. Older and more worn primaries will result in a shorter wing measurement and should be noted.

Weight—Because bird weight varies substantially with geographic population, condition of the individual, and season or period within the life cycle of each particular species, this measurement is not as useful for ageing, sexing, or identifying birds as is the wing chord. Weight, however, is an important indicator of the health of the bird, especially when coupled with wing length and fat content. It should always be recorded, when possible, to the nearest tenth of a gram.

Molt

Types of Molt—Relatively little is known about the timing, sequence, and extent of molt in many species, especially in Latin America. A proper understanding of molt can be extremely helpful in the accurate ageing and sexing of passerine birds in the hand. With a few known exceptions, molting is confined to two periods within the annual life cycle of North American passerine birds, just before and just after the breeding season.

USDA Forest Service Gen. Tech. Rep. PSW-GTR-144-www. 1993.

17

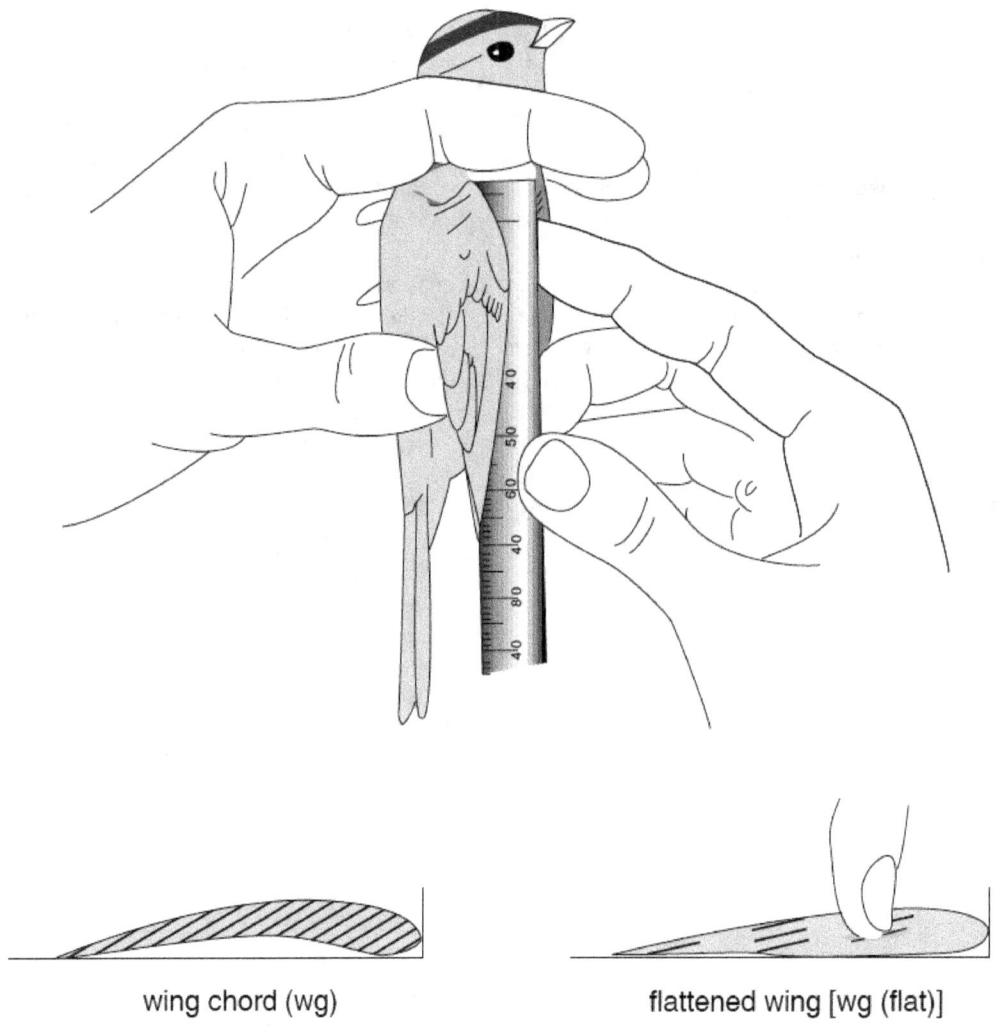

wing chord (wg)

flattened wing [wg (flat)]

Figure 8—Above, a good hold for measuring the wing chord, and below, the measurement of the wing chord and flattened wing. The wing chord is preferred in North America. Taken from Pyle and others (1987).

Thus, most adult passerine birds display two plumages, the basic (winter) plumage and the alternate (summer or breeding) plumage. The molt that occurs just before the breeding season is called the prealternate molt; that occurring just after the breeding season is the prebasic molt. All North American passerine birds have a prebasic molt, and just over half (predominantly migratory species) have a prealternate molt.

The prebasic molt usually occurs from July to September on the breeding grounds and occurs in both recently fledged birds and adults that have completed nesting activities for the year. With one or two exceptions, the prebasic molt in adult passerine birds is "complete" (fig. 9; includes all body and flight feathers), whereas hatching year birds of most species typically replace the body feathers and some coverts, but not the primary coverts, and flight (wing and tail) feathers (except the central two tail feathers) during a "partial" first prebasic molt.

As you blow apart the feathers on the various areas of the body, you can easily determine which feathers are molting by the presence of a cylindrical sheath around the base of the molting feather. When the feather is fully grown, this sheath

is preened off and the feather ceases its traffic with the body and is thus fully grown.

Birds have three types of flight feathers: the rectrices, or tail feathers, and the outer (primary) and inner (secondary) wing feathers. The rectrices are numbered in pairs, beginning with the central ones (the "decks") as #1, and proceeding outward in both directions usually to #5 or #6, depending upon the taxon. In some species the decks are sometimes molted by the young at the same time as their body feathers. The remaining rectrices molt in an ascendant sequence from #2 through #6.

The secondaries are long flight feathers attached to the skin at the ulna, the bone of forearm. These are numbered by all authors beginning at the bend of the wing and proceeding inward toward the body. This is the usual order of molt, except that the three innermost secondaries (tertials) molt like body feathers and may be molted by juveniles. They are also often molted concurrently with the longer secondaries.

The primaries are the long flight feathers attached to bones of the "hand." These are numbered in most of the North American literature from the wrist-joint (bend of the

18

USDA Forest Service Gen. Tech. Rep. PSW-GTR-144-www. 1993.

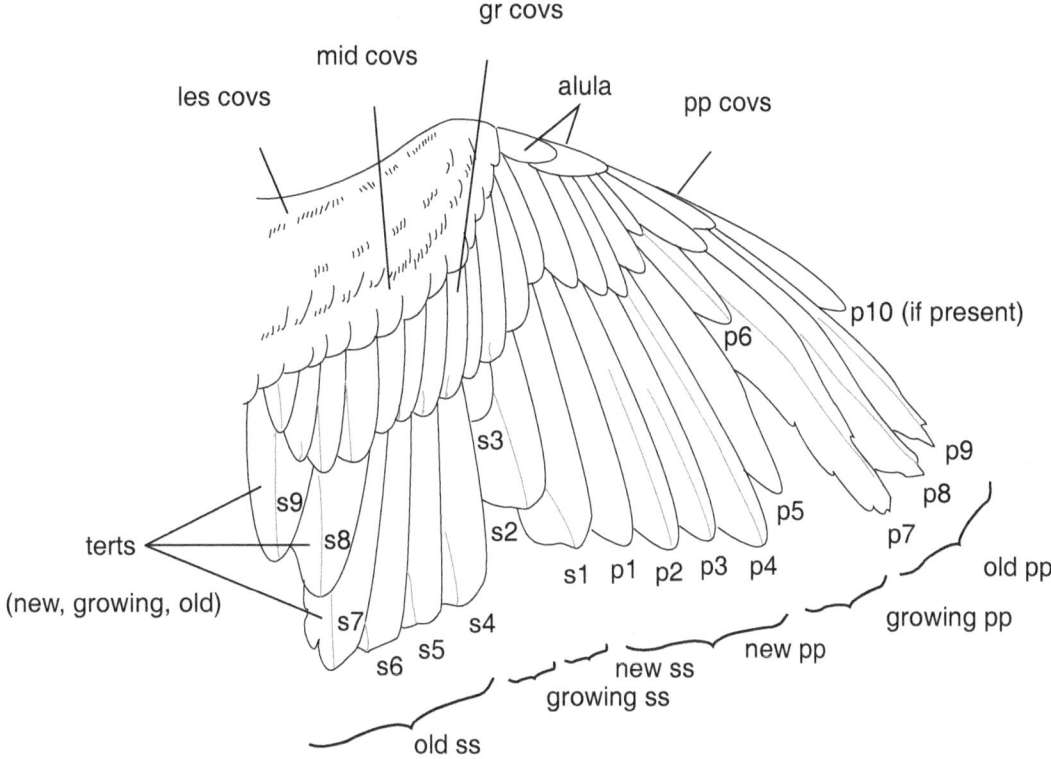

Figure 9—An example of a wing during complete molt of an adult. Notice the worn primaries 7-9 and secondary 7. Taken from Pyle and others (1987).

wing) outward, which is the sequence that nearly all birds molt these feathers.

Pyle and others (1987) have provided a complete enumeration of the numbers of flight feathers of passerine birds in North America.

Recording Molt—A basic system of recording molt in the flight feathers is to record presence or absence of molt in the primary feathers or the secondaries (except the innermost three). We suggest that the molt in the tail feathers not be recorded, except as a note. You should always check both wings, because birds often lose feathers accidentally ("adventitious molt"). Flight feather molt is "**S**" if symmetrical and normal, "**A**" if adventitious, and "**N**" or "**0**" if none.

More detailed recording of molt can be conducted using the British Trust for Ornithology's method (Ginn and Melville 1983).

Body molt can be recorded by a subjective determination of none (**N** or 0), trace (**T** or 1) (a few, perhaps adventitious molting feathers), light (**L** or 1) (involving more than one feather tract), medium (**M** or 2), or heavy (**H** or 3) molt.

Extent of Juvenal Plumage

We suggest that the extent of juvenal plumage be recorded, because it is a good indicator of the age of a young bird and the timing of breeding. Juvenal plumage can be coded in the following: **N** or 0 = no juvenal body plumage; **L** or 1 = less than half of juvenal plumage remains; **H** or 2 = more than half of the juvenal plumage remains, some first basic plumage is visible; **F** or 3 = full juvenal plumage, bird has not started first prebasic molt. For a more objective measure, the bander could estimate the percent of juvenal plumage.

Primary Feather Wear

Feather wear could be a useful indicator of age, because it seems likely that the juvenal generation of flight feathers may wear faster, and thus show more wear at any given time, than later, adult generations of feathers. Faster wear results from the rapid growth of juvenal feathers resulting in weaker feathers, and the protracted molt of adults. In some species during especially the early breeding season, adult flight feathers, molted after the previous breeding season, are much older than juvenal feathers and can help age birds.

Examine the outer four or five primaries to determine wear, and classify them according to the following scale: **N** or 0 = No wear, the feather edges are perfect, and the entire edge is light, including the tips; **S** or 1 = **S**light wear, the feather edges are slightly worn with no fraying or nicks, and the edge is often light-colored, except at the tips; **L** or 2 = **L**ight wear, the feathers are definitely worn, but with little fraying and few nicks; **M** or 3 = **M**oderate wear, considerable wear with definite fraying, and nicks and chips are obvious along the edges; **H** or 4 = **H**eavy wear, feathers very heavily worn and

USDA Forest Service Gen. Tech. Rep. PSW-GTR-144-www. 1993.

19

frayed, and the tips often worn completely off; and **X** or 5 = Excessive wear, feathers are extremely ragged and torn, the shafts are usually exposed well beyond the vane, and all the tips are usually completely worn or broken off (one wonders how well the bird can fly).

Fat

The amount of fat on a bird may indicate periods of stress, low availability of food, low fledging weight, and other conditions that give insight into the viability of an individual. Especially as birds prepare for migration, subcutaneous fat is accumulated and is visible beneath the skin as white, yellow, or light orange areas easily seen in contrast to the red muscular areas. The fat can be most easily seen on the abdomen and the furculum. The furcular or interclavicular region is the depression formed between the attachments of the pectoralis muscles to the furculum (the "wish-bone") and coracoids, forming a "V" running toward the spinal cord and pectoral girdle, through which the neck protrudes. You can assign a fat class on the basis of how much fat you can find:

Fat Class	Furculum	Abdomen
N or 0	No fat, the region is concave	No fat
T or 1	Trace, deeply concave, scattered patches, less than 5 percent filled.	None, or a trace
L or 2	Thin **Layer**, less than a third filled.	Trace or thin layer
H or 3	One-**Half** filled in small patches covering some areas.	Small patches, not
F or 4	More than 2/3 Filled, level with clavicles	Covering pad, slightly mounded
B or 5	Slightly **Bulging**	Well mounded
G or 6	**Bulging Greatly**	Greatly distended mound
V or 7	**Very** large fat pads of furculum and abdomen meet	

Data Entry

We include a standard data form *(fig. 10)* that we encourage you to use. Fill in all the information, and print neatly in soft, black pencil. For codes not shown, and for exact definitions, see CWS and USFWS (1991). Right justify data in appropriate fields. Do not use ditto marks. If data are repeated on the next line, use a slanting line in the field from upper left to lower right, or a vertical line in the center of each column. If data are not collected, leave the column blank, or enter 9's for numerical data. If a band is lost or destroyed, indicate this in the code column and also in the species column. On any one sheet place only the records for one band size or the recaptured birds. When starting a new series of bands, or a new calendar year, **always** start a new banding sheet. The sheet is broken into the following categories:

• Heading material: State code, region code, band size ("R" for recaptures, entered on a separate sheet), page number (for each band size), and year of banding or capture.

• Recorder and bander—Place the initials of the recorder and bander here, and their full names at the bottom of the page (these are not entered into the data base).

• Code—This column tells if it is a: new banding (**N**); recapture (**R**) (a bird previously banded); unbanded bird (**U**) (place 9's in the band number columns); destroyed band (**D**); lost band (**L**); or a changed band (**C**) (a band that replaced an old or worn band—make a note of the old band number).

• Band number—The full, right-aligned number of the first band on the first line. Thereafter, the final three digits of new bands only. Do not use dashes in this field to separate prefix; rather, right align all numbers. On recapture pages, the full band number should be entered each time.

• Species—An abbreviation of the species name (e.g., Bl-cap Chick, for Black-capped Chickadee). The abbreviation is not entered into the data base, but is a check against the error-prone species codes below, such as Barn Swallow (BARS) and Bank Swallow (BANS).

• Species Code—The four-letter code of species name (e.g., BCCH). The list of these for North America is in CWS and USFWS (1991). A Latin American version has not yet been prepared, but biologists can use the first two letters of the genus and the first two letters of the species names. This will suffice for many species.

• Age—The single letter or numeric codes as indicated above.

• How aged—Use the following codes: **A**, adult plumage; **B**, brood patch; **C**, cloacal protuberance; **E**, eye color; **F**, feather wear; **H**, hatching year (first winter) plumage; **I**, inside of mouth or any part of bill; **J**, juvenal plumage; **M**, molt; **P**, plumage in general; **S**, skull; **T**, tail length; **W**, wing length; or **O**, other (explain this code in the Notes section). Write the codes in their order of importance to your age determination.

• Sex—Use M for male, F for female, and U for unknown.

• How sexed—Use the codes as in "how aged."

• Skull—Record the code above that indicates the percent of skull pneumatized.

• Cloacal protuberance—Use the code described previously

• Brood patch—Use the code described previously.

• Fat—Use the codes described previously.

• Body molt—Use the codes described previously.

• Flight feather molt—Use the codes described previously.

• Flight feather wear—Use the codes described previously.

• Juvenal plumage—Record the extent of this plumage, using the codes described previously.

• Wing length—Record to the nearest millimeter.

• Weight—Record to the nearest tenth of a gram.

• Status—Among the most common are: 300, normal and released; 301, color-banded; and 615, injured and released. The full list of status codes is in CWS and USFWS (1991).

• Date—Month, day, and year, all in numbers.

• Capture time—Using the 24-hour clock, record to the nearest 10 minutes, e.g., 6:24 a.m. is 062, 4:48 p m. is 165, etc.

• Station/location—Record an abbreviation using four letters for the station's name and two numbers for the net location; a total of six columns used.

• Notes—Record any useful additional data, such as: sequence of color bands, if present; suspected ages or sexes of birds coded "U"; information on unusual wing lengths; or why an "other" code was used for how aged. If additional data are taken, such as an unusual age category, they should be placed in the "Notes" columns, in order to keep primary data consistent.

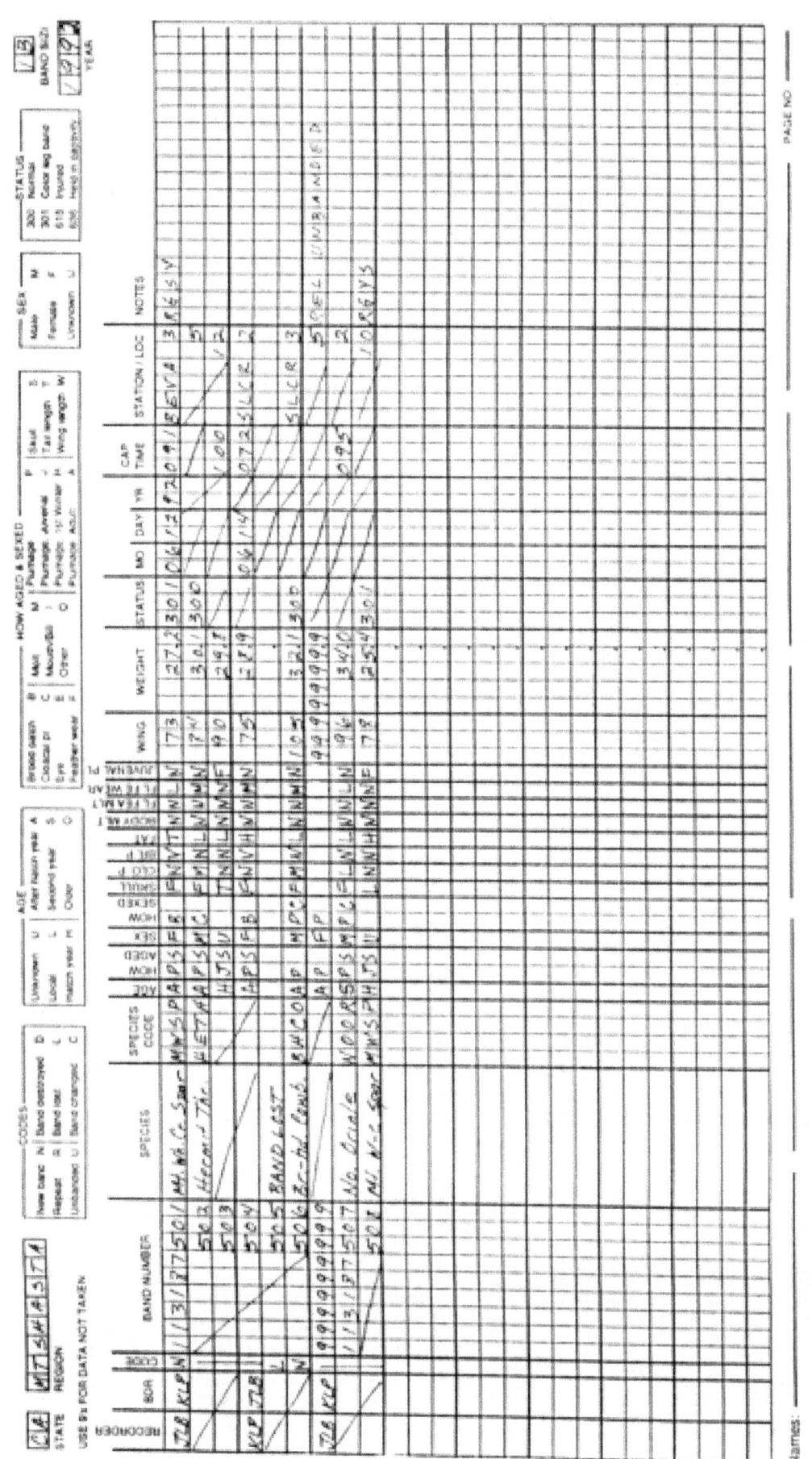

Figure 10—An example of a form for recording data from captures.

USDA Forest Service Gen. Tech. Rep. PSW-GTR-144-www. 1993.

21

Sources of Equipment[1]

Advertisements for supplies and good articles on capture techniques can be found in the publication "North American Bird Bander." Persons doing mist netting or banding should join their regional Association and receive this, the joint publication of the Western Bird Banding Association (BBA), 1158 Beechwood St., Camarillo, CA 93010 (Colorado and west); Eastern BBA, R.D. #2, Box 436A, Hellertown, PA 18055 (Appalachians and east); or the Inland BBA, 81 Woodshire Drive, Ottawa, IA 52501.

Mist Nets

Nets can be purchased in the United States at the following:

Association of Field Ornithologists, c/o Manomet Bird Observatory, Box 936, Manomet, MA 02345 [telephone (508) 224-6521]. A wide assortment of nets.

Avinet, P.O. Box 1103, Dryden, NY 13053 [telephone and FAX: (607) 844-3277]. They have a wide selection of nets, banding tools, scales, poles, color bands, and other material.

Eastern Bird-Banding Association, Gale W. Smith, R.D. #2, Box 131, Kempton, PA 19529. An assortment of nets.

Color Bands

The only source of split-ring plastic color bands for landbirds that we have found is A.C. Hughes, Ltd., 1 High Street, Hampton Hill, Middlesex TW12 1NA, England. Avinet (see above) carries a limited supply of Hughes' bands.

The best bands for most species are the "Plastic Split Rings" in solid colors. We have found their five most visible and separable colors are Red, Yellow, Light Blue, Dark Blue, and Orange. If more colors are needed, some investigators have found White reasonably separable from the standard aluminum band, and the Black and the Dark Green separable from the Dark Blue. Hughes' sizes (and their Fish and Wildlife Service approximate equivalents) are: XF (0), XCS (1), XCL (1B), XB (1A), and X3 (2).

Optical Device for Skulling

An excellent one is OptiVisor, a binocular magnifier available in 2.5, 2.75 and 3.5 powers. Available from the manufacturer Donegan Optical Company Incorporated, P.O. Box 14308, Lenexa, Kansas 66285-4308, or call them at (913) 492-2500 for a distributor near you.

Wing Rulers

Rigid tempered steel rules with a stop at the end are very good for measuring wings. Sizes are 15 cm, 30 cm, and 60 cm. Available from Chris N. Rose, 98 Lopez Rd., Cedar Grove, NJ 07009.

---

[1] The use of trade or firm names in this publication is for reader information and does not imply endorsement by the U.S. Department of Agriculture of any product or service.

Banding Pliers

The best have holes in jaws to fit standard U.S. band sizes, with a split pin on top for even band opening. Three pliers are available: one will open all of band sizes 0, 1, 1B, and 1A; another for sizes 2 and 3; and one for sizes 3B, 3A, and 4. These are available from Roger N. MacDonald, 850 Main St., Lynnfield, MA 01940, (617) 334-3448.

Scales for Weighing

Electronic scales are widely available for under $300, and Pesola scales and a spring balance field scale are available through Avinet (see above). A good general purpose one has a capacity of 300 g and a readability of 0.1 g. The Ohaus C-Series costs under $200 and Acculab has one under $150. With a capacity for most birds, Acculab has a pocket balance with 80 g capacity for under $100. These are available from many scientific supply houses, such as Markson, P.O. Box 3944, Houston, Texas 77253 (800-528-5114).

Bags for Holding Birds

Washable bags can be made, or cotton mailing bags can be purchased. An ideal size for most small birds is 6 by 9 inches, or somewhat larger. U.S. Government agencies can purchase excellent cotton mailing bags from the General Services Administration.

Bird Banding Laboratory and Office

All capture work must be done under very strict regulations and permits. Permit applications in the United States can be obtained from the Bird Banding Laboratory, U.S. Fish and Wildlife Service, Laurel, Maryland 20708. In Canada, the address is Canadian Bird Banding Office, Canadian Wildlife Service, Environment Canada, Ottawa, Ontario K1A 0H3. Special permits are also needed from most states and provinces, and the above offices can supply information on them. Many Latin American countries also require permits.

The Bird Banding Laboratory and Office provide excellent support for all activities relating to capture, and permittees receive bands at no cost. However, they have limited resources for supporting banding work and cannot honor all requests for permits. Applicants for permits must show evidence of qualifications and must have a well-justified need to band. Permittees are expected to provide accurate and timely reports of birds banded.

Nest Searches

Nest searches provide the most direct measurement of nest success in specific habitats. They also allow identification of important habitat features associated with successful nests and insight into habitat requirements and species coexistence. Knowledge of the appropriate cues and techniques for finding nests allows large numbers to be found, thereby providing vital information about many species. Nest searches have an advantage over constant-effort mist netting, in that the measures of success are direct and habitat-specific. However, they are more limited as to the area surveyed and do not measure individual survivorship. Mist nets sample birds from a larger area, and the data derived may therefore have wider applicability, but are not habitat specific.

In this section we describe aids and standardized techniques for locating and monitoring success of nests, adapted from Martin and Geupel (in press).

Nest Sites

Nest finding is labor intensive (DeSante and Geupel 1987, Ricklefs and Bloom 1977), but most observers can improve their ability to locate nests in a matter of days with training and practice.

The behavioral observations and clues described below work effectively for a variety of species. However, our experience includes a small subset of species and habitats and, in particular, is largely restricted to forest and shrub habitats. Other methods may be more effective in other habitats. For example, cable-dragging (Higgins and others 1969) and rope-dragging (Labisky 1957) may be more effective for many grassland species. In particular, all species, and even some individuals, differ in nest placement and behaviors near the nest. The patience and alertness of observers, and their familiarity with the habitat and behavior of individual species, are the most important influences on effectively locating nests.

Nest finding can be a frustrating task; patience is an important asset. It is a good idea to set a goal of finding at least one nest daily. More than one nest will be found on many days, but if at least one nest can be consistently found every day, the numbers of nests over the season will rapidly accumulate.

Methods

The particulars of plot sizes and numbers will vary according to the purpose of the study or activity, the habitat involved, and the density of birds. As a general guideline, we recommend that two study plots be established for each person that searches for nests. The searchers should work alternating days on these two plots for the entire nesting season. This provides consistent monitoring and allows the person to become familiar with the plot. In general, eight plots, each 40-50 ha, would usually be necessary to be established in forest habitat to find sufficient numbers of nests (ca. 20 nests per species) for the range of species typically found in any given forest, but smaller plots (ca. 10 ha) can be established in areas with higher densities.

In general, one should try to develop as quickly as possible a search image for the nests of various species. T. Sherry (pers. comm.) notes that he routinely finds 25-50 percent of his nests by constantly scanning appropriate potential nest locations in the vicinity of an active female.

During Nest Construction

Ideally, nests should be located during construction to provide the best estimates of nest success. This is also usually the easiest time to find nests because of the high level of activity and, in some areas, forests are not leafed out, making the task of following the female much simpler (T. Sherry, pers. comm.). We advise biologists to spend the maximum amount of time early in the season when the finding rate is maximum. Nest building begins by May in most areas of North America, although permanent residents and some ground-nesting species will begin earlier. Only the female constructs the nest and incubates the eggs for most small terrestrial birds (Kendeigh 1952, Silver and others 1985). Exceptions include woodpeckers, vireos, and wrens. Thus, the most effective way of finding most nests is by locating and following females, although males may provide some cues. Some nests in the shrub layer can be found by random search. Ground nests in forests are usually the most difficult to find. It is best to watch the female as she is gathering nesting material without using binoculars, because when she flies, she can be followed more easily with the naked eye.

Females tend to be extremely furtive during nest building. A mated female can be recognized by copulations or by her movements around the territory unharassed by the male. Females should always be checked with binoculars, especially during and after long, direct flights, to determine whether nesting material is being carried. Many birds will carry very fine material, not obvious upon casual inspection, such as spider webbing and hair for lining nests.

Sitting near sources of nesting material (e.g., failed nests, thistles) or open areas with a good view of the territory can help detection of nest-building females. Observers should use different paths across plots to increase the probability of randomly encountering females near undiscovered nests.

Follow a bird with nesting material from a distance to avoid disturbance. Do not interrupt a long flight. If the bird disappears in a patch of vegetation, begin to scan for potential nest sites. Be patient and wait for another visit by the bird. If the area where the female disappears is near the nest, the female will spend time in the area. At the same time, be aware that the female may move out of the back side of the patch to another patch that contains the nest.

Some individuals tolerate nearby observers and behave normally, but most species are very wary of observers. If the observer is too close to the nest, the bird often will sit on a perch somewhere near the nest site until the observer leaves. Eventually the bird will drop the nesting material if the observer does not move away. Thus, such behavior is an indication that the observer is too near the nest and should move quickly away. Obtain a new position at some distance (ca. 15 m) hidden by vegetation. Observe the female arrive with nest material and leave without it from the same location several times. Be aware that a female can skulk into one patch of vegetation and leave unobserved to move to a different patch, then return the same way, to give the appearance of nesting in the first patch. Some species such as MacGillivray's Warbler, Hooded Warblers, and Sage Sparrows will walk on the ground for several meters to approach the nest secretly. Birds can often be detected by watching for movement of the vegetation where they are otherwise hidden. Where the vegetation stops moving is usually the nest site.

USDA Forest Service Gen. Tech. Rep. PSW-GTR-144-www. 1993.

23

Mapping the male's position as he sings around the territory can often reveal a center of activity from which the male can often see the nest (T. Sherry, pers. comm.). The observer then can scan appropriate nest sites nearby, or at least increase the chance of catching a glimpse of a wary female.

Once the suspected nest site has been identified, back away quickly. Verify the status and location a few hours later, being careful that the female is absent. Do not approach the nest while the female is watching; disturbance at this early stage can cause abandonment. After quick verification, the area should be left and not visited for four days.

During Egg-Laying

This is the most difficult stage for finding nests because the female may visit the nest only when she lays an egg, and most species lay one egg per day. The female will sometimes sit on the nest during egg-laying when weather is particularly harsh. Nest visitation becomes more frequent with more eggs in the nest (Kendeigh 1952).

Behavioral cues are useful at this stage. When either parent gets near the nest, they will look at it. If an egg-laying female detects a predator in the area, such as an observer following her, she will sometimes check the nest. Another good cue is a female staying in an area without actively feeding. She will often look at the nest site repeatedly, aiding location of the nest.

Finally, copulatory behavior can be used during both nest-building and egg-laying. Copulation often occurs in the same tree above a nest, on the same branch, or in the next tree. Examine carefully the area immediately adjacent to copulatory activity.

During Incubation

The beginning of incubation can be estimated as when females suddenly "vanish," and males increase singing. Some behavioral cues can help locate nests. Females start foraging faste during the incubation and nestling stages, probably because their time is more limited. Females that are making rapid hops, quick short flights, and rapid wing flicks will probably return to the nest soon. On average, most passerine females are off the nest for 6-10 minutes and on for 20-30 minutes (e.g., Zerba and Morton 1983).

Observers can find females by alertly moving through the study plot, but sitting down in a spot for 20-30 minutes is also useful. A female leaving a nearby nest can thereby be detected. Females can also be detected by call notes, although species differ in the types of sounds. Females of many taxa (e.g., gnatcatchers, warblers, Emberizine finches) chip or call just before leaving, or just after leaving, the nest. This behavior seems to be a communication note to the mate. Females of other species use other vocal signals, e.g., thrushes give a chuck or mew sound; tanagers often give a characteristic sound near the nest or during copulation; and some taxa (e.g., Emberizine finches and icterines) have a nest departure call (McDonald and Greenberg 1991), often answered by the male. If you detect, follow, but then lose a vocalizing female,

immediately return to the original location where she was detected, and you may often find her again before she returns to the nest.

Males can also be of some help. When the female is off the nest, some males quietly guard the nest or follow her (for example, the Gray Catbird) (Slack 1976). A quiet male may indicate presence of a foraging female or a nest nearby. In many species, especially cavity-nesters, males will feed incubating females (e.g., Lyon and Montgomerie 1987; Martin and Geupel, unpubl. data; Silver and others 1985). Males of some species (e.g., Chestnut-sided Warbler) use singing perches that are in direct view of the nest. Males sitting on a perch, looking towards the same spot, may indicate a nest.

Males can sing anywhere in the territory while a female is incubating, but he can become silent when the female is about to leave, or has left, the nest (T. Sherry, pers. comm.). When this occurs, he will often make a long flight over to where the female is starting to forage (and sometimes will incite her to leave the nest). Sherry suggests being alert to these flights because they provide valuable clues to where the nest vicinity is, and can also help the observer detect females, which are often difficult to find considering how long they stay motionless during incubation.

A female foraging off the nest is fairly tolerant of people, but observers should be inconspicuous. As she returns to the nest, she is more cautious. This can be used to an observer's advantage. First, a relatively long flight after foraging is probably a return to the nest, and is often along the same route. Quickly running in her direction for about 25 m may often result in a resighting, because the disturbance will keep her from returning to the nest, giving more time to relocate her. If she is near the nest, but cautious about approaching, she will bounce between a few branches, and may also forage rapidly. Eventually, she will start to move down toward the nest several times and then suddenly fly back up, apparently indecisive. If the observer is too close to the nest, the bird will continue to bounce, and will sometimes fly off, only to return within a few minutes. The observer should then back off and watch. If it is cold, do not keep her off the nest for too long. If the female has been followed for more than 30 minutes without results, then she probably is not on a nest, unless both sexes incubate.

If a female disappears into a tree or shrub, the nest is probably in or next to it. Memorize the area where the female disappeared and choose potential nesting sites before approaching. Moving quietly, begin tapping potential nest shrubs with a stick. Listen for the flush of the female off the nest. If unsuccessful, the site can be revisited for careful searches.

In many species, nest site preference seems to be an evolutionarily conservative trait (Martin 1992). Some birds greatly prefer their nest to be in or under certain plant species, or in particular patch types (Martin and Roper 1988, Martin unpubl. data). Describe and visit nest sites from previous years to aid new observers in finding nests.

During the Nestling Stage

Finding nests during the nestling period is the easiest,

because both males and females commonly bring food and remove fecal sacs. Males are normally the easiest to follow, as they tend to be less cautious. Nests can usually be found from a distance using binoculars because of the constant activity of the parents.

In some species a singing male can indicate the nest location. He may sing, for example, less and less as he starts to gather food to carry to the nest, become silent when he is about to approach the nest, and then resume loud song immediately after leaving the nest (T. Sherry, pers. comm.). Additionally, Sherry notes that birds will often become reticent to go to a nest with a human nearby, so that if a bird becomes relatively inactive (hopping around, not taking long flights) in a particular area, or dropping prey, then the nest is probably nearby. In this case, the observer should either search intensively in the vicinity, if likely nest spots are nearby, or back away to give the bird a chance to become calm and go to the nest.

Knowledge of the nesting cycle allows an observer to anticipate when to start looking for a new nest. Most species will renest after a nesting failure, although this varies among and within species (Geupel and DeSante 1990a, Martin and Li 1992). Reconstruction usually begins within 10 days, and the earlier in the nesting cycle that failure occurred, the farther apart the nests are likely to be (citations in Martin 1992). Multi-brooded species may renest in as little as 8 days after fledging. Sometimes the female will begin nesting while the male is still tending the fledglings of the previous brood (Burley 1980).

Nest Monitoring

Each nest found needs to be checked every 3 to 4 days to determine its status. Careful attention to checking nests is critical for data quality, because the number of days that nests have eggs or young is used to calculate daily mortality rates, the most effective measure of nest success (Mayfield 1961, 1975). Nests should be checked from a distance the day before expected fledging, and every other day thereafter. A chart showing nests as they are found and the expected date of fledging is extremely helpful. If nestlings appear ready to fledge before the next scheduled visit, then the next visit should be sooner. Calculations of nest success should terminate with the last day that young were observed in the nest. Nests should also be checked more frequently about the time of hatching, if the length of the incubation period is desired.

With canopy nests, mirrors attached to telescoping aluminum poles can check contents of nests. These are available from stores stocking swimming pool supplies, and are commonly up to 4-5 m. A window-washing pole to 12 m is also available (Tucker Manufacturing Company, 613 Second Ave. S.E., Cedar Rapids, Iowa 52406; 319 363-3591). T. Sherry (pers. comm.) suggests a convex mirror to allow views from a variety of angles from the ground. Mounting a small flashlight next to the mirror can illuminate the nest contents in cloudy or rainy weather. Often binoculars must be used to view the nest in the mirror.

Careful and detailed observations should be recorded if a nest predation event is observed. If the nest appears inactive from a distance, it should be approached to verify. If the eggs or young appear to be gone, then check the nest structure and immediate area, perhaps up to 6-10 m (T. Sherry, pers. comm.) for evidence. Any evidence (e.g., shell fragments, hole in nest, nest torn up) should be fastidiously noted. When the young fledge, they commonly perch on the edge, flattening it, and leave fecal droppings in (or on the edge of) the nest. These would indicate possible successful fledging. Observers should try to verify success by seeing fledglings or by hearing adult alarm calls or begging calls of the young. Fledglings normally do not move very far in the first couple of days, although some, such as Rufous-sided Towhee, may move 100 m in a few hours. Some species or individuals may carry food up to 24 hours or longer after predation of their nest, including to unrelated fledglings from neighboring territories.

Nestlings may be banded when the primaries first break sheath. Banding may provide valuable information on juvenile survival and dispersal. Always have an assistant with you to record data, and be careful the nestlings do not jump out as you try to remove them (use two hands). Avoid banding in the morning or during cold or wet periods.

Filling Out the Forms

Two types of data sheets are used to record data about the nest site and nest activity. One set ("Nest Check Form"—*fig. 11)* is used in the field to record information when nests are checked. To prevent loss, and serve as a backup and summary record for each nest, the "Nest Record Form" *(fig. 12)* should be maintained at some permanent location. The Record Form should be updated daily, to prevent data loss.

All observations should be recorded on the Check Form and transferred to the Record Form, including visits with no activity. This is particularly critical for canopy or cavity-nests where nest contents cannot be viewed.

Nest Check Form

Data are collected in the field and are recorded on the Check Form. One to several nests can be recorded on a single form. When a new nest is found, its location is carefully noted at the bottom of the form, and the form may be needed in the field over the next few visits to relocate the nest. The data taken should include:

• State or province—The 2-column code for each.

• Region—An 8-column code, designated by the investigator. Often, the name of the USGS quad, a prominent landmark, or a nearby town will provide the best code name.

• Station—A 4-letter code for the station that contains the nest search plot.

• Year.

• Observer's initials.

• Nest number—A unique, identifying 2-column number for the nest site. We would expect that at each station, for each species, no more than 100 nests would be found.

USDA Forest Service Gen. Tech. Rep. PSW-GTR-144-www. 1993.

25

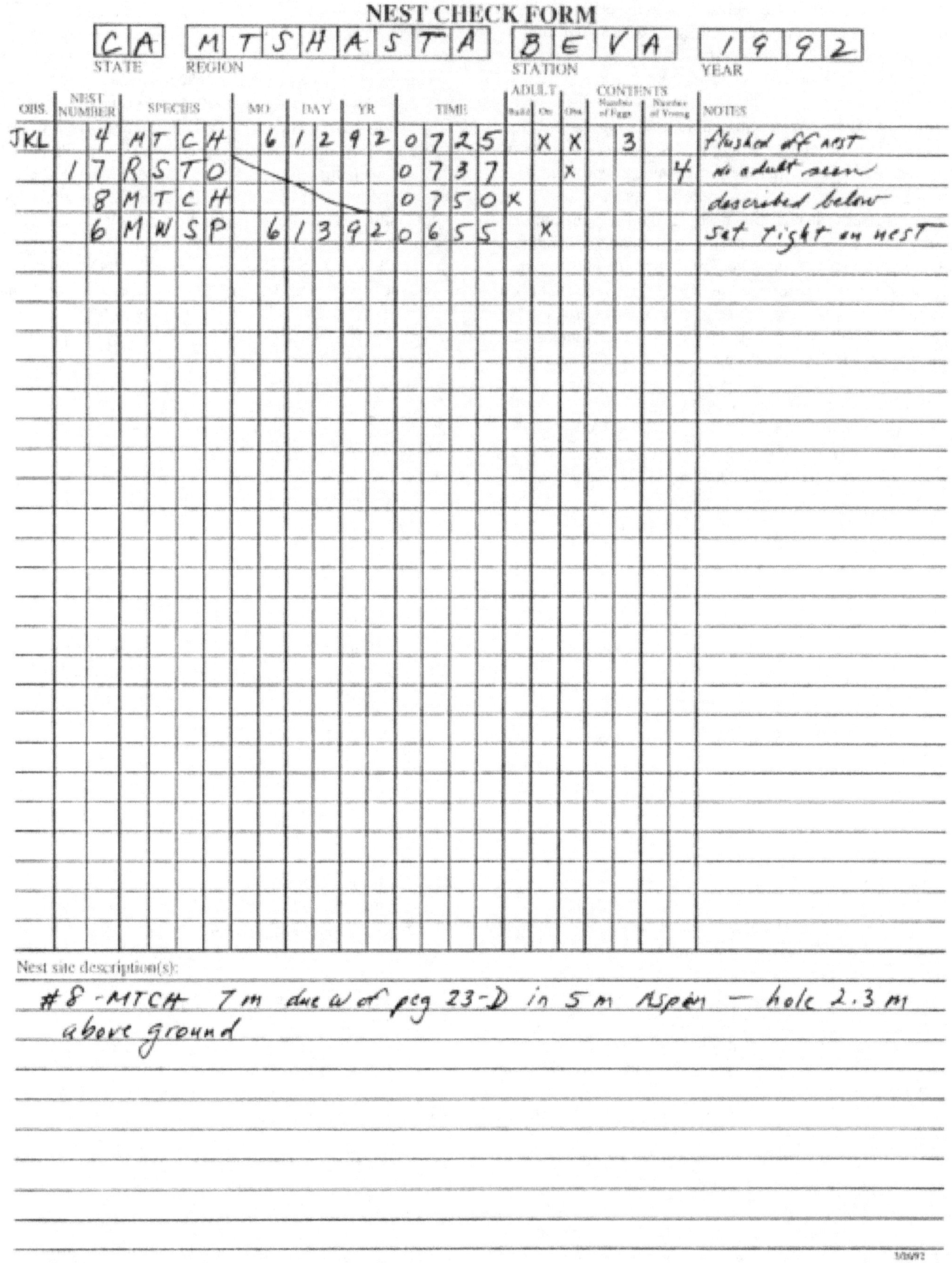

NEST CHECK FORM

STATE	REGION	STATION	YEAR
C A	M T S H A S T A	B E V A	1 9 9 2

OBS.	NEST NUMBER	SPECIES	MO	DAY	YR	TIME	ADULT Build	ADULT On	ADULT Obs	CONTENTS Number of Eggs	CONTENTS Number of Young	NOTES
JKL	4	M T C H	6	1 2	9 2	0 7 2 5		X	X	3		flushed off nest
	1 7	R S T O				0 7 3 7	X		X		4	no adult seen
	8	M T C H				0 7 5 0	X					described below
	6	M W S P	6	1 3	9 2	0 6 5 5		X				set tight on nest

Nest site description(s):

#8 - MTCH 7m due W of peg 23-D in 5m Aspen — hole 2.3 m above ground

Figure 11—An example of a Nest Check Form for recording in the field the status of nests and information on where the nest is located.

USDA Forest Service Gen. Tech. Rep. PSW-GTR-144-www. 1993.

NEST RECORD FORM

1.

C A		M T S H A S T A		B E V A		M T C H		1 9 9 2		4	2
STATE		REGION		STATION		SPECIES		YEAR		NEST NO.	ATTEMPT

2. NEST CHECKS

DATE		CONTENTS					COMMENTS
Month	Day	Build ing	Adult on	obser ved	Number of eggs	Number of young	
6	6	X					entering hole
6	9	X		X			3/4? built
6	12		X	X	3	0	flushed off nest
6	15			X	3	0	
6	18			X	0	0	empty

DATE		CONTENTS					COMMENTS
Month	Day	Build ing	Adult on	obser ved	Number of eggs	Number of young	

3. DATES and PERIOD

Month	Day		Contents
6	6	Found	start of nest
6	9	1st egg	Number
6	12	Clutch completion	3 eggs
		Hatched	nestl.
		Fledged or failure	fledg.
6	15	Last date active	

Outcome *predation - jay ?*

Cause of failure P E

Period	Number of days observed	Success
Egg laying	4	5
Incubation	3	D
Nestling	0	

4. NEST SITE

Measurements in cm unless otherwise designated

Plant common name *Alder*

Genus

A	L	N	U	S						

Plant height	5 3 0	Nest height above ground 2 7 0
Plant dbh	4 5	Nest dist. from edge 3 2
Canopy cover (denso.)	6 0	Nest dist. from center/stem 0
Number support branches	0	Diameter support branches
Concealment from above		from below
Concealment from side N	S	E W
Compass direction		Total % cover nest substrate

Band numbers of young

USDA Forest Service Gen. Tech. Rep. PSW-GTR-144-www. 1993.

27

Figure 12—An example of a Nest Record Form that is kept at a permanent location for recording data from the Nest Check Form, as well as the nest site and characteristics data.

- Species name—The 4-letter code, based on CWS and USFWS (1991).
- Date—Month, Day, Year.
- Time—Use the 24-hour clock.
- The activity of an adult if either building ("build.") or incubating ("on"), by putting an "X" in the blank.
- The observer should record the contents of the nest whenever it is approached close enough for careful observation. If the contents are actually observed, this should be noted by an "X" in the observed box ("obs."). If the contents are counted accurately, the number of eggs, young, or both, are noted. Age of the nestlings should be estimated when possible because it can help determine the nest fate by providing information on length of time that nests were active. Age estimates should be recorded in Notes.

The form also includes space for a description of one or more nest sites that the observer finds on this day. The description should be sufficiently detailed to allow anyone to locate the nest. Take compass readings from a fixed point (e.g., a stake or grid point) to establish a reference location.

Nest Record Form

This form is filled out each day upon return from the field, and should contain the following data:
- Header data
  State or Province
  Region
  Species code
  Year
  Nest number
  The number of attempts at nesting that this record represents for that pair for that season.
- Nest Checks. These are the data transcribed from the Check Form, and are the same as for that form.
- Dates and Period
  The following dates should be tabulated, as they become available: date of finding of nest (and contents when found), date of first egg laid, date of clutch completion (and number of eggs laid in final clutch), date of hatching of last egg (and number of nestlings produced), date of fledging (and the number of fledglings), or nest failure, and date when last active.
  Outcome, a written description of the fate of the nest.
  Cause of failure (codes: UN = unknown because not revisited; FY = fledged, with at least one young seen leaving or in vicinity of nest; FP = fledged young, as determined by parents behaving as if dependent fledgling(s) nearby, FU = Suspected fledging of at least one young, but uncertain (e.g., no adult behavior observed); FC = fledged at least one host young with cowbird parasitism; PO = predation observed; PE = probable predation, nest empty and intact; PD = predation, damage to nest structure; AB = nest abandoned prior to eggs; DE = deserted with egg(s) or young; CO = failure due to cowbirds; WE = failure due to weather; HA = failure due to human activities; and OT = other).

Period = the number of days nest was observed for the following: days during the egg laying, incubation, and nestling period.
Success = for each period, based on the following codes: S = **S**uccessful, D = **D**epredated, N = status unknown/nest **n**ot occupied, U = status **U**nknown/nest occupied fate unknown, M = **M**ortality other than predation, A = **A**bandoned, F = **F**emale died, Z = abandoned, no (**z**ero) eggs laid.

Predation Risk from Monitoring

Locating and monitoring nests have potential to increase predation (Major 1989, Picozzi 1975, Westmoreland and Best 1985). With proper precautions, such biases can be eliminated or minimized (Gottfried and Thompson 1978, Willis 1973). Finding the nest normally creates the most distress to adults and disturbance to the nest site because subsequent visits are brief. Some evidence suggests that predation rates are higher on the first or early visits than subsequent visits (Bart 1977, but see Bart and Robson 1982).

Therefore, we suggest the following when locating nests:
- Minimize distress calls by adults; never allow them to continue for more than five minutes;
- Do not approach a nest when any potential nest predators, particularly visually-oriented predators (e.g., corvids), are present;
- Minimize disturbance to the area around the nest; and
- Do not get close to nests during nest building, as birds will abandon if disturbed before egg-laying, particularly during the early part of a season.

To lower the probability of predation or brood parasitism from checks, we recommend that you
- Check from as great a distance as possible, using binoculars to look into the nest or climb up to look from above;
- Approach nests on different paths on subsequent visits, using paths that are quick, quiet, and that minimize vegetation disturbance;
- Never leave a dead-end trail to the nest, but continue walking in a different direction;
- If avian predators are common, check other bushes without nests, and always assume a predator is watching;
- Be quick and accurate during nest checks and nestling banding;
- Minimize the number of observers;
- Use a pen or stick to check nests to prevent human scent from being left on or near a nest.

Vegetation Measurement

We suggest two methods of vegetation measurement: (1) the nest and the plant containing it; and (2) the nest site and random points in the plot. The entire plot should be measured with a series of points, as outlined in the section "Methods of habitat assessment" below.

The Nest and Nest Plant

Measurement of the vegetation of the nest site is an important research tool and has some application to monitoring. If you wish to determine this aspect of habitat, we suggest that you measure the vegetation as soon as a nesting attempt terminates. Be careful at the beginning of the season, as an empty nest may not yet have eggs. Some species or individuals will delay laying as long as eight days after completing nests. Do not delay measuring the vegetation, because foliage density around the nest changes rapidly.

We suggest the following measurements *(fig. 12)*, of the plant containing the nest. All measurements should be in centimeters.

- Plant species common name.
- Plant species genus.
- Plant height.
- Nest height.
- Plant "dbh" (diameter at breast height), stem diameter of the nest substrate, usually measured at 0.25 m above the ground, because many nests are in substrates less than "breast height."
- Nest distance from edge—Distance from edge of plant, inward to the nest.
- Canopy cover—The canopy cover at chest height should be measured using a densiometer. This is a measure of the tree canopy, and should be measured as close to the nest as possible, but not under the canopy of the nest plant if it is a shrub.
- Nest distance from center/stem—Distance of the nest laterally from the main stem.
- Number of support branches—The number of branches actually supporting the nest.
- Diameter support branches—Average diameter of stems supporting the nest.
- Nest concealment—Measured by estimating percent of the nest concealed by foliage cover in a 25-cm circle centered on the nest from a distance of 1 m from above (overhead cover), from below, and from the side (side cover) in each of the four cardinal directions.
- Compass direction—Direction from the nest to the main stem of the substrate.
- Total percent cover nest substrate—The percent cover of the plant containing the nest, using the outer margin of the plant as the boundary. This is most useful in shrubs.

The Nest Site and Random Points

Vegetation in the patch surrounding the nest can provide information on differences in microhabitat choice among species.

We recommend using vegetation sampling methods based on a series of points, as outlined in the section "Methods of habitat assessment," below, or those described in Martin and Roper (1988) with some modifications (obtainable from Martin). The point method involves measuring habitat features in the nest patch in circular releves of 11.2-m radius centered on the nest, smaller than the 25- to 50-m releves for general

habitat assessment, detailed below. In addition, non-use sites should be sampled with the same protocol at 35 m from the nest in a direction parallel to the contour of the plot (to stay within the same microhabitat type when possible). The sampling plot should be centered on the plant stem nearest to the 35-m point that is of the same species and size as that used for the nest. Random plots can also be established in a grid to obtain a stratified random sample of the vegetation. Comparisons of random versus nest plots can indicate choice of microhabitat types. Comparisons of nest versus non-use plots then provide information on choice of habitat patches within a microhabitat type. These sampling protocols keep the methods relatively compatible with other sampling schemes (e.g., James and Shugart 1970), but also allow tests of hypotheses about the interactions between choice of nest site and predation risk or habitats chosen for nesting.

Censusing

The assessment of population size should be an integral part of any monitoring program. Various methods have been employed and thoroughly tested (see Ralph and Scott 1981). Abundance of birds has long been used to measure habitat suitability but is often retrospective, giving trends without any possibility of determining causation, and can even be misleading (van Horne 1983).

It is desirable to use a method that allows the biologist to census as many points as possible in the time available, thus gaining as many independent data points as possible. That is, it is much better statistically to census five points in a 10-day interval, than to count at one point five times. The farther apart each of the five points, the more likely the data can be extrapolated to a larger region.

Below we outline four major methods. Two of these, the point counts and the spot mapping methods, are the most common ones used (for definitions see Ralph 1981b). The point count is probably the best for most surveys and has been adopted as the standard method for monitoring (Ralph and others, in press). The methods for both are taken in part from the excellent book by Koskimies and Vaisanen (1991). In addition, a strip transect count and an area search method are also presented. The latter is especially popular with volunteers.

General Considerations
Time of Day

The best time for censusing at most temperate latitudes during the breeding season is usually between 5 and 9 a.m. Under most circumstances, no counts should be done after 10 a.m. Exceptions could be in the non-breeding period. It is best to start within 15 minutes of local sunrise. Examining pilot data is the best way to determine when detection rates are the most stable. In general, the period between official sunrise and the ensuing 3-4 hours is usually relatively stable. For most species, during the period between dawn (first light) and

USDA Forest Service Gen. Tech. Rep. PSW-GTR-144-www. 1993.

29

sunrise, the number and rate of birds singing is somewhat higher than the rest of the morning. For maximum comparability in detection probabilities for species among points, it will be best to start at sunrise rather than at first light.

Census Period

Breeding season point counts should be run during the time of year when the detection rates of the species being studied are most stable. Within the breeding season, the months of May, June, and the first week in July are best for counting most passerines in North America. However, stable counting periods, when the rate of singing of the various species has stabilized, are as early as April in the Southeast and Southwest and may extend later in the boreal zones. In Latin America the breeding season will be longer, and censuses can profitably be conducted throughout the year.

Weather

Birds should not be surveyed when rain or wind interfere with the intensity or audibility of bird sounds, when fog or rain interfere with visibility, or when cold weather shuts down bird song activity.

Point Counts

We suggest two levels of point counts. **Extensive point counts** are intended for a series of points, placed at a minimum of 250 m apart, largely on roads or trails over an entire region. **Intensive point counts** are placed within a mist net or nest search plot.

The account below is based on Hilden and others (1991), and the standards are taken from Ralph and others (in press), as adopted by the Point Count Workshop of the Monitoring Group of the Neotropical Migratory Bird Conservation Program, held in Beltsville, Maryland, November 1991.

Background and Aims

In many countries point counts are the main method in monitoring the population changes of breeding landbirds. With the point count method it is possible to study the yearly changes of bird populations at fixed points, differences in species composition between habitats, and abundance patterns of species. The point count method is probably the most efficient and data-rich method of counting birds. It is the preferred method in forested habitats or difficult terrain. Point counts involve an observer standing in one spot and recording all the birds seen or heard at either a fixed distance, or unlimited distance. This method can be conducted one or many times at a given point. The North American Breeding Bird Survey of the U.S.D.I. Fish and Wildlife Service is such a method.

The point count method applied to landbirds does not provide reliable data on waterfowl; however, rails and waders are counted well. Some landbirds also pose problems as they are particularly quiet, loud, nocturnal, or flocking. If these species are of particular interest, the method may be modified to accommodate them.

Equipment and Time Needed

One should not start point counts without good identification skills, including a knowledge of the songs and calls of birds. Details on training for distance estimates are given in Kepler and Scott (1981). In the tropics, learning all the songs and calls of all species at all times of the year is difficult in practice. In many areas it takes an experienced observer 4-8 weeks to identify 80-90 percent of the species. In temperate zones, this can often be done in less than 2 weeks.

For the census one needs a map, a pencil, notebook, a watch that shows seconds, and binoculars. The route and the points are marked on a survey map and, if necessary, in the field with plastic tape or streamers to ensure that the same points are found in the following years. The observer may move from one point to another by foot or with a vehicle.

The time needed for censusing one point count route is usually no more than four morning hours, depending on the distance between the points and the method of travel.

Choosing a Counting Route for Extensive Point Counts

An extensive point count route should encompass all the habitats of a region, if possible. In addition, it should include any mist net or nest searching plots in the region. In choosing a route and laying out the points for census, use a systematic rather than random sampling design, either on roads or off roads. Systematic gridding of points is preferable to the random placement of points in most cases. Systematic placement can include placing points at designated distances along roads. Do not stratify by habitat, unless separate estimates for a habitat are required. If the goal is to estimate population trends for an entire management unit, then point counts should be spaced evenly throughout that unit, or along the road system in an area, without regard to current habitat configurations.

Observers should attempt to carry out censuses primarily on tertiary roads, then secondary roads, and should avoid wide, primary roads. Off-road censuses should be carried out on trails, if possible, in major habitats not covered by road systems. Using roads, travel time can be reduced to as little as 1-2 minutes between sampling points. Under optimal road conditions, up to 25 5-minute point counts can be conducted in one morning. In an off-road situation, the number of point counts one observer can conduct during a morning varies between 6 and 12. Roadside habitats usually do not sample all of the available habitats. In this situation, a collection of both on- and off-road surveys can be created that best fits local conditions. Although a road modifies the surrounding habitats, we feel that tertiary road systems (i.e., narrow dirt roads) allow for birds to be counted in approximately the same proportions as off-road surveys.

The minimum distance between point counts in wooded habitats is 250 m. Birds previously recorded at another sampling point should not be recorded again. In virtually all habitats, more than 99 percent of individuals are detected within 125 m of the observer. In open environments, this minimum distance

30

USDA Forest Service Gen. Tech. Rep. PSW-GTR-144-www. 1993.

should be increased because of the greater detectability of birds. Along roads, where travel by vehicle is possible, distances of 500 m or more should be used.

Choosing Points for Intensive Point Counts

The intensive point counts are conducted within a study plot for mist nets or nest searches. We suggest between 9 and 16 points in a grid of 3 by 3, 3 by 4, or 4 by 4 points. For most analyses, the birds counted from these points will be combined into a single mean. Therefore, the distance between points is less critical than for extensive point counts where each point is intended to be statistically independent. The points on an intensive census grid should be adjusted to fit within the netting array or nest search plot so as to fully census the area. It is very important not to include areas much beyond the array or plot boundaries. These are covered by the extensive point count censuses. For example, a census grid of nine points, 100 m apart, would cover 4 ha. Allowing for an effective radius of censusing of perhaps 50 m outside this grid, the area covered expands to about 9 ha. A grid of 12 points 150 m apart would have an effective area of about 22 ha. Thus a census grid should have points that are between 75 and 150 m apart, depending upon the area to be covered and the number of points to be included. Under most circumstances 9-12 points should be more than adequate.

Field Work

The censuser should approach the point with as little disturbance to the birds as possible. Counts should begin immediately when the observer reaches the census point. Time spent at each count point should be 5 minutes if travel time between counting points is less than 15 minutes (for greater efficiency) and 10 minutes if travel time is greater than 15 minutes. If a survey is primarily for inventory and few points will be surveyed, then 10 minutes is appropriate. Data should be separated into those individuals seen or heard during the first 3 minutes (for comparison with Breeding Bird Surveys) and those additional individuals heard in the remaining 2 and 8 minutes.

The details of each point are recorded: the reference number, name of the point, date, and the time. The species are written down in the order they are observed. For each species, the number of individuals is recorded separately for those within a circle of 50 m around the censuser and for all those outside the circle, out to an unlimited distance. In noisy environments, dense foliage, or in tropical forests, observers have found that 25 m was preferred. The distance is that at which the individual was first observed. For birds near the 50-m border, the category may be confirmed by measuring paces to the border when the counting is over. If a bird flees when the censuser arrives at the point, the bird should be included according to its take-off place. Birds that were detected flying over the point, rather than detected from within the vegetation, should be recorded separately.

Estimating distances requires experience, so a new censuser should measure the length of steps in different terrain, and then check the distance to several singing birds in order to make the estimating of distances routine. Estimating may be eased by either natural or artificial landmarks.

If there are several males of the same species around a point, one may sketch in the margin the directions and distances of each singing male with an arrow to ensure that they are not confused. Juvenile birds or birds that fledged during the current breeding season should be recorded separately.

A bird flushed within 50 m of a point's center as an observer approaches or leaves a point should be counted as being at the point if no other individual is seen during the count period. It is advisable that this be recorded separately.

If a flock is encountered during a census period, it may be followed after the end of the period to determine its composition and size. An observer should follow such a flock for no more than 10 minutes. This is especially useful during the winter. A bird giving an unknown song or call may be tracked down after the count period for confirmation of its identity.

No attracting devices or records should be used, except in counts for specialized groups of birds.

Filling in the Forms

The data taken at point counts are of two types, the location information and the census data. The location data are contained in the first three lines of the "Location and Vegetation Form" (fig. 15, described below) and contain information about each census point. We also suggest that the vegetation data be taken (see Habitat Assessment, below). We suggest two types of census data forms. One involves mapping and the other direct recording.

Mapping Point Counts—This method of taking data involves the recorder placing on a map (fig. 13) the location of each bird detected (D. Welsh, pers. comm.). We suggest that species codes be used on the map, with a single letter for the most common species, and the full 4-letter code for other species. The birds' activities can be recorded by the various mapping symbols given in *figure 13*. The circle on the map can be the 50-m radius, enabling the observer to keep track of individuals easily. The orientation of the observer ("DIR") should be entered on each form by placing the compass direction in the box at the top. Separate time periods are easily kept by using different colored pencils, e.g., birds seen in the first 3 minutes in black, and those seen within 3-5 minutes in red.

The data are then transcribed onto the Point Count Data Form (fig. 14), described below.

Direct Recording Point Counts—This method involves a single-step process of the observer recording the observations directly on the Point Count Data Form (fig. 14). Many observers do not think that it is necessary to map the location of birds in order to keep track of individuals. Using this method, an observer tallies in pencil each individual detected by placing a "tick" mark (a single line), or another code, in the appropriate column. Codes, for example, can be used to separate out singing vs. visual-only birds (S and V) and age categories. When field work is over, the actual number in each distance and time category can be written in ink for data entry.

POINT COUNT LOCATION MAPPING

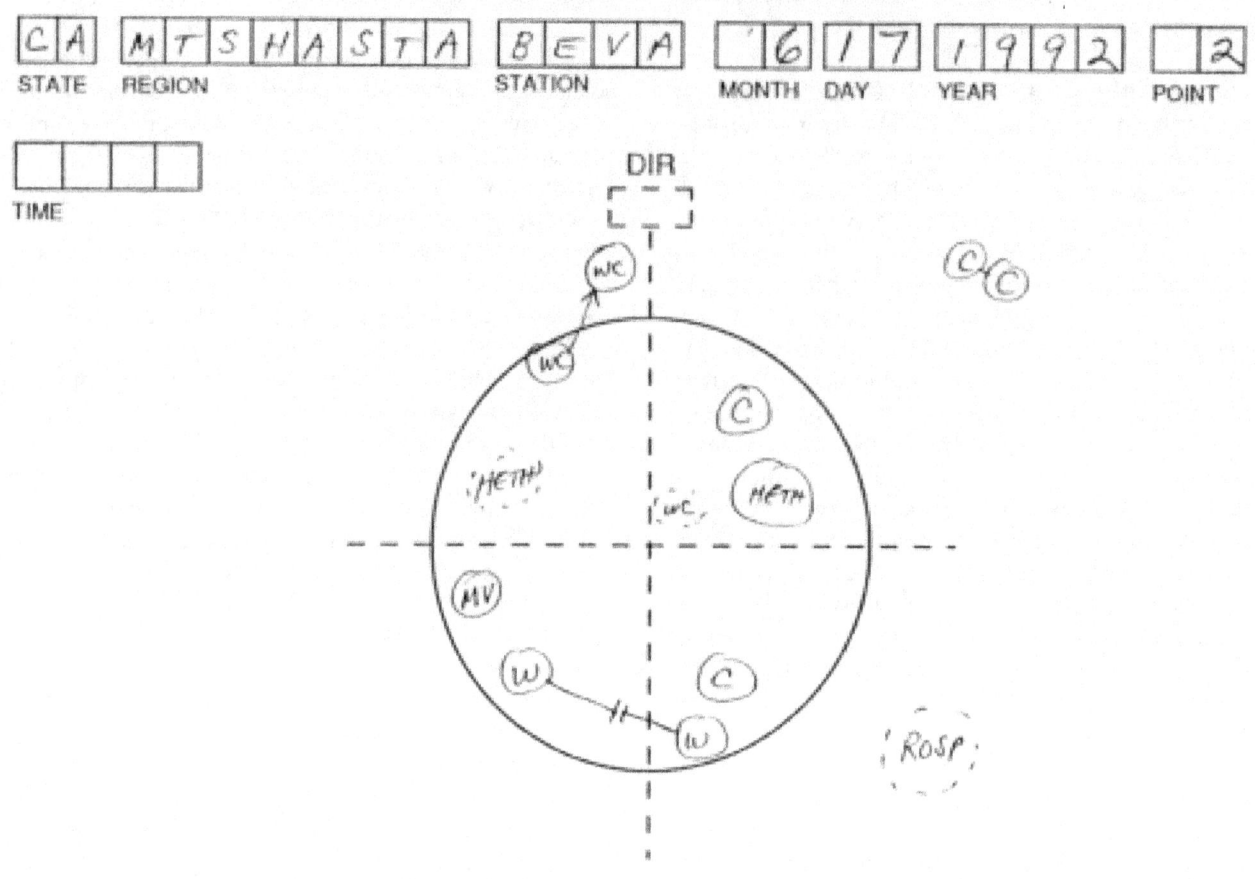

C	A		M	T	S	H	A	S	T	A		B	E	V	A			'6		1	7		1	9	9	2			2

STATE   REGION   STATION   MONTH   DAY   YEAR   POINT

TIME

MAPPING SYMBOLS

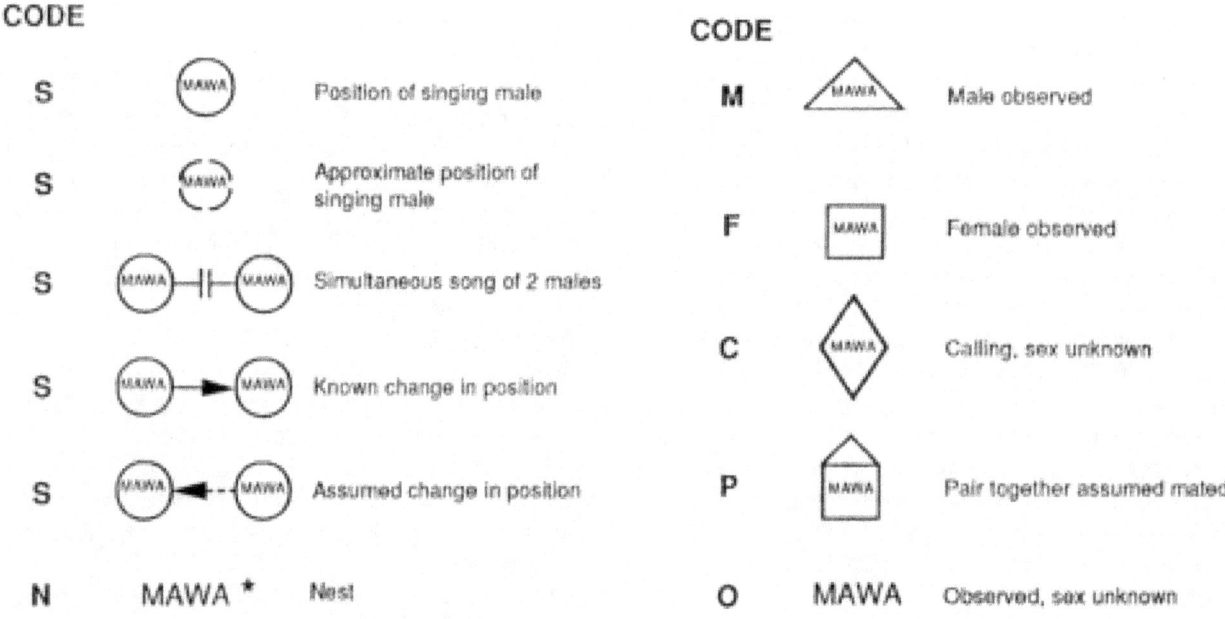

Figure 13—A recording form for mapping the location of birds during point counts with some mapping symbols. Taken from Welsh (pers. comm.)

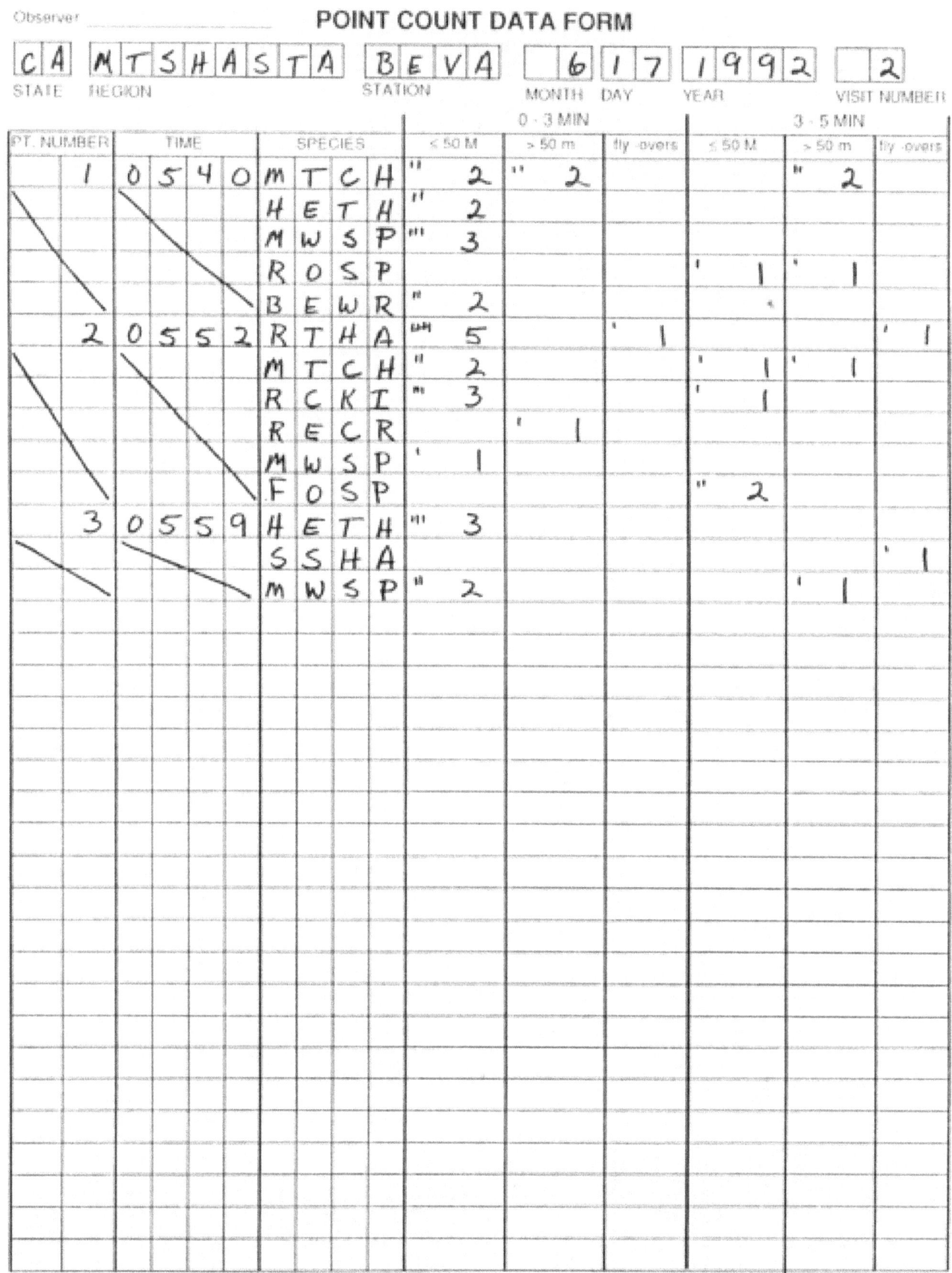

Figure 14—An example of a data form for recording point count data. Birds are recorded separately within or outside a 50-m circle around the observer, and in the first three minutes or later in the census. The data are recorded as "tick" marks in each box; then later the actual numbers of birds, as derived from the data, are summarized and recorded.

LOCATION AND VEGETATION FORM

LOCATION

STATE	REGION	STATION	LOCATION / POINT	MONTH	DAY	YEAR
C A	M T S H A S T A	B E V A	5	1 0	1 2	1 9 9 2

LATITUDE 4 0 6 3   LONGITUDE 1 2 2 0 9

ELEVATION (M)	ASPECT	% SLOPE	WATER	PLOT RADIUS (M)	NOTES
2 1 3 0	1 8 7	3 2	+	2 2	LARGE (5m) ROCK NEAR CENTER

VEGETATION

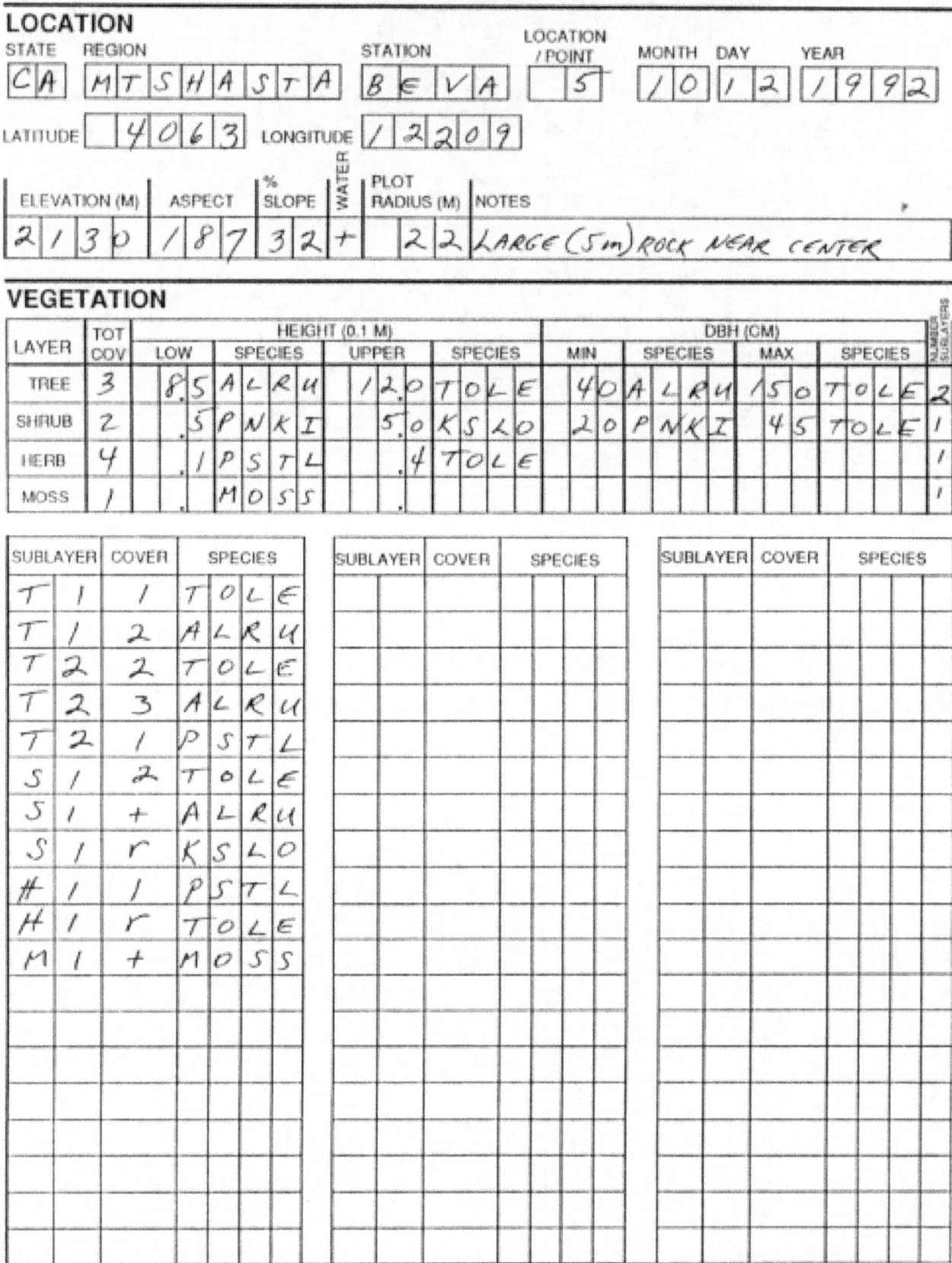

LAYER	TOT COV	HEIGHT (0.1 M)					DBH (CM)					NUMBER SUBLAYERS
		LOW	SPECIES	UPPER	SPECIES		MIN	SPECIES	MAX	SPECIES	
TREE	3	8.5	A L R U	12.0	T O L E		40	A L R U	150	T O L E	2
SHRUB	2	.5	P N K I	5.0	K S L O		20	P N K I	45	T O L E	1
HERB	4	.1	P S T L	.4	T O L E						1
MOSS	1	.	M O S S	.							1

SUBLAYER	COVER	SPECIES				SUBLAYER	COVER	SPECIES				SUBLAYER	COVER	SPECIES
T	1	1	T O L E											
T	1	2	A L R U											
T	2	2	T O L E											
T	2	3	A L R U											
T	2	1	P S T L											
S	1	2	T O L E											
S	1	+	A L R U											
S	1	r	K S L O											
H	1	1	P S T L											
H	1	r	T O L E											
M	1	+	M O S S											

Figure 15—The Location and Vegetation Form. The upper portion should be filled out at all study locations. The bottom portion quantifies vegetation.

The specific data suggested are as follows:
- State or province—The 2-column code for each.
- Region—An 8-column code, designated by the investigator. Often, the name of the USGS quad, a prominent landmark, or a nearby town will provide the best code name.
- Station—For intensive point counts, we suggest a 4-letter code, the same as that used for the mist net array or nest search plot. For extensive point counts, we suggest a code relating to the general area or road. In general, we expect that a given station will have no more than 50 points.
- Month, day, and year.
- Observer
- Visit number—Indicate how many visits this year will have been made to these points at the end of this day's census.
- Point Number—The 2-column census point number.
- Time—Using the 24-hour clock.
- Species—The 4-letter species code.
- Tally of individuals—This is a series of five fields. The major subdivisions are those birds detected at less than, and more than, 50 m, and those birds flying over, but not landing within detection of, the observer. Within the two distance categories, observers can separate out those detected in the first three minutes, and the next two minutes. Observers wishing to separate out behavioral, age, or sex categories can note them with an appropriate letter code. Otherwise, "tick" marks (e.g., 3 = ///) can be used.

Repeating the Count

In general, a station should be sampled only once each season. Counts can be repeated if the goal is good estimates of the community at certain, specific points, such as a small area of rare wetland habitat.

The timing of the census of each route should be kept constant from year to year; it should not differ by more than seven days from the date of the first count. If the phenology of the spring differs, then the date can be changed. The start of the count should not differ by more than 30 minutes from that of the first year. If possible, the same observer should census the route every year.

Strip Transects

Strip transects are very similar to point counts, but the observer records all birds seen or heard while traversing each section of a trail. Each section is then the unit of measurement, and can be 100 m or 250 m long. This method is best used in very open terrain where the observer can devote his or her full attention to the birds, and not worry about footing.

In this method the observer should attempt to cover a given amount of trail in a fixed amount of time, e.g., 100 m in ten minutes.

Area Search
Background and Aims

The area search method has been adopted for a nation-wide survey, the Australian Bird Count (Ambrose 1989), and was chosen over several others because of its appeal to volunteers.

It uses a method that, while quantitative, mimics the method that a birder would use while searching for birds in a given area. Essentially this is a series of three 20-minute point counts in which the observer can move around in a somewhat restricted area. In this way unfamiliar calls can be tracked down and quiet birds can be found.

Preparation

The observer should be reasonably familiar with most (if not all) bird species likely to be encountered at the plot. This method allows the observer to track down unfamiliar birds, but walking the plot before a survey with a person familiar with the birds allows the observer to be more efficient.

Choosing a Plot

The plot should allow relatively easy detection and identification of birds (by sight or calls) and allow the observer to move about freely. The plot should be sufficiently large to provide three separate search areas (or plots), each about 3 ha in forest or dense woodland, but larger areas of 10 ha or more can be used in more open habitats. In very dense forest, smaller areas of 1-2 ha can be used. The search areas can have adjoining boundaries or can be in completely separate regions of the plot. More than three search areas can be established within a plot, but the same search areas must be used on each visit.

Time of Day

Because of the intensive nature of this method, it can be carried out longer into the morning than other methods. However, it should continue no later than five hours after dawn.

Field Work

Walk throughout the plot for exactly 20 minutes in each search area, stopping or moving to investigate sightings or calls when appropriate. Record numbers of birds of each species seen, heard, or both seen and heard in the search area during this time. Record birds outside the search area separately, but concentrate on finding as many birds as possible within the plot. The observer may find it easier to tape record observations and then transfer results onto paper soon after the survey. An accompanying person can serve as a recorder. A single survey is completed after at least three areas have been searched at a plot.

Filling in the Form

A standard form is suggested, listing the species found and a running tally of the number of birds, both on and off the area. These tallies can be totaled on the right of each area for each species.

Spot Mapping
Background and Aims

The mapping method is based on the territorial behavior of birds. By marking the locations of observed birds on a detailed map during several visits within a breeding season, it is possible to count the number of territories in an area and estimate the density of birds. Spot mapping is not usually used as a general method for broad-scale monitoring of breeding landbirds, because it requires more time and field work than single-visit point counts and line transects. However, the method should be applied when fairly precise pair numbers and densities as well as the distribution of territories in small study areas or patchy habitats are to be studied. The standard mapping method is less suitable for species that live in colonies or loose groups, or species with large or no territories.

In general, one or two observers make repeated visits (a minimum of 8) to specific plots during the breeding season. Some habitat analysis is also required. Standard methodology as described by Robbins (I.B.C.C. 1970) is also used by The Cornell Laboratory of Ornithology's (CLO) resident bird counts. The latter program, known as the "Breeding Bird Census" (BBC), is a continent-wide program that welcomes contributors and publishes results of North American plots annually in the *Journal of Field Ornithology*. The CLO also encourages "Winter Bird Population Studies" (WBPS) on the same plot. For more information, write to: CLO, Resident Bird Counts, 159 Sapsucker Woods Road, Ithaca, NY 14850; Telephone (607) 254-2441. The basics of the method are contained in Koskimies and Vaisanen (1991). We present here enough information for a biologist to evaluate the technique. The methods of especially data recording, evaluation, and analysis are complex and detailed.

Equipment and Time Needed

One needs 30-40 copies of a very detailed map (preferably 1:2000, or, in open areas, 1:3000 may be acceptable), a compass, and flagging for marking the area.

The time needed depends on the size and terrain of the census area as well as on bird density, with higher densities requiring the mapping of more individuals. Usually about 10-30 hectares in a wooded area or 50-100 ha in an open area may be counted in one morning. Thus, in forest it takes 10 mornings to census 30 ha by the ordinary 10-visit version of the mapping method (about 50-60 hours of field work). In addition, it can take as many as 40 hours (4 hours per census morning) to prepare the species maps, and about 5-10 hours to analyze them. In total, one could spend as many as 100 hours censusing 30 ha of forest during one breeding season. Marking the 50-by 50-m plot in the field takes about 25 hours before the first census season.

Drawing a Map and Marking the Area

The census area should be as round or square as possible in order to minimize border length, because territories along edges are difficult to analyze. After the area has been chosen, a detailed map (known as a visit map) is drawn of it before the first census. The recommended scale for the map is 1:2000. A survey map (1:20,000) and field experience should be used in drawing. Boundaries of the area and landmarks such as edges between habitats, streams, roads, paths, buildings, big rocks, and trees are marked on the map. There should be enough landmarks on the map so that the observer can locate the positions of birds accurately on the map. One copy of the map is needed for each visit, and enough copies should be reserved for making the species maps. If there are only a few natural landmarks, a grid of 50-m squares can be established with the corners of the squares marked with plastic flagging with coordinates written on them.

Census Period and Number of Visits

Because of differences in phenology of arrival and nesting, the visits should cover a period long enough to ensure that each species is easily observable on at least three visits. There should be 10 visits in a standard mapping of forest birds. If the bird density is very high and the nesting period of the community is long, 12 visits are recommended. The visits ought to be evenly distributed over the census period. Fewer visits can suffice in open habitats, where bird densities are usually lower than in forests, or where the season is short (e.g., tundra or alpine grasslands).

Time of Day

The main census time is 5 a.m. to 10 a.m. when the birds sing most actively. After a very cold night counting can be delayed. During very warm weather it should be prolonged because of the lower activity of birds. Two visits should be made in the evening: the first in the beginning of the census period (especially for counting thrushes), the second about two or three weeks later (especially for counting nocturnal singers). If there are several nocturnal or dusk-active species breeding in the area, these two censuses should be added to the ordinary program of 10 morning visits, for a total of 12. In northern temperate zones, owls, woodpeckers, and crossbills breed early and should be censused by extra visits in March and April.

Field Work

A clean map is reserved for each visit. Each visit should cover the area as evenly as possible, and no place should be farther from the route than 25 m (dense vegetation or high density of birds), 50 m (sparse vegetation, few birds) or 100 m (open habitats). The route you follow through the plot should be on a grid twice the size of the distances above, for example, 50 m in dense habitat. Successive visits should be started at different points, especially if you think that a part of the area is getting attention at the expense of the rest. Simultaneous observations of two individuals of the same species singing or seen must always be recorded carefully so that birds can still be separated from their neighbors after they have moved, which frequently happens during a census visit.

Even while you are busy censusing, you should not walk very slowly, because then, for example, a bird uttering alarm calls may attract other birds to congregate nearby. Therefore, walk with moderate speed and record the birds all the time. Stop frequently to "hunt" for simultaneous observations of different individuals of the same species, to listen, and to mark the birds on the map. If you are not sure whether there is only one bird or two, you can return to the area censused already to make sure which is the case. In open areas it is often useful to search for the birds with binoculars.

36

The ordinary speed of censusing is 10-12 min/ha, or 5-6 ha/hour when the bird density is about 300-500 pairs/km². If the density is very high, the censusing speed slows down to 3-4 ha/hour (15-20 min/ha). When the density is very low or only some of the species are being censused early in the spring, one may walk a little more rapidly; however, at least eight minutes should be allowed for each hectare.

There are many advantages to slow and thorough censusing: (1) one can gather simultaneous observations effectively by following the movements of individual birds in different parts of their territories; (2) one can pay special attention to species difficult to detect; and (3) one can search for nests and check those found earlier. All observations are marked on a map using standard codes which are given in the detailed instructions in Koskimies and Vaisanen (1991). All observations are transferred from the field maps to exactly the same locations on the species-specific maps. There should be a separate map for each species.

Other Considerations

Color Banding Individuals

Observer variability can be a great problem in many of the censusing schemes described above (Verner and Milne 1989). The color banding of individuals allows field identification and survival estimates of individuals without recapture and can greatly enhance spot mapping efficiency, the ability to find nests, and basic life history information. Furthermore, it allows more detailed observation of behavior including breeding biology, survival, and foraging ecology. Color-banding and other auxiliary markers must be authorized by the Bird Banding Laboratory.

Methods of Habitat Assessment

Many applications of habitat analysis are in the literature (e.g., Verner and others 1986). It is not our intention to outline what analyses can be done, but to emphasize that, at the least, vegetation information should be taken at each of the stations. Objectives of vegetation assessment can be many, but among the most common are to relate, in one way or another, the changes in bird composition and abundance to differences in vegetation. These vegetation changes can be either changes over time, or differences between habitats. Two adequate, but relatively time-consuming, methods of habitat assessment are those of James and Shugart (1970), used primarily in forested habitats, and Noon (1981). An excellent and rapid method which could be substituted for the method of estimating stand characteristics below is that of MacArthur and MacArthur (1961) which involves estimating foliage density. The technique uses horizonal measurements to estimate density by relating the percentage of a board that is obscured by foliage. This method has been tested and found reliable by Conner and O'Halloran (1986) and Conner (1990).

If managers wish to characterize the interactions of birds and habitat in a region, then some kind of habitat classification with sampling in proportion to the relative abundance of habitat in that region is the optimal design. This sampling, stratified by habitat, should be done with the guidance of a biometrician.

We present two alternatives here. One is that used to type vegetation into broad habitat classifications, as the Constant Efforts Site vegetation assessment technique does, or a more specific one, involving estimation of stand characteristics. We strongly suggest the latter method, as being more useful for monitoring.

Broad Habitat Classification

Objectives—This method provides brief, overall classification of vegetation and a map that allows other investigators to evaluate the habitat of your station. These data should be the minimum collected on vegetation at any monitoring station. If more detailed vegetation data are collected, then this level need not be taken.

Considerations—The information collected should provide enough data to determine the vegetation types. The method will not provide quantitative information for correlative analyses and ordinations.

Procedures—It is best to make a map of the main areas of habitat within the station on a yearly basis, sometime in June. Prepare it on the scale of approximately 1:2000 (approximately 1 foot to a half mile [1 m to 2 km]). Include the major vegetation types, extending it at least 100 meters beyond the outermost net or capture location. Indicate on the map: trails, roads, ditches, streams, marshy areas, net or census points, open water, and broad habitat boundaries. Also on the map should be a reference point identifiable on a U.S. Geological Survey topographic map or equivalent.

Use colored lines to separate habitat types, and record the following on a form:

• Habitat type: broad category such as forest, brush, marsh, field, etc.

• Shrubby vegetation: list the shrub species comprising more than 10 percent cover in order of their percent cover in each type.

• Trees: list the tree species comprising more than 10 percent cover in order of their percent cover in each type.

• Height of vegetation: record the approximate average height of the canopy of forest or brush to the nearest meter.

• Ground layer: describe the vegetation of the ground layer in terms of the common name of the main species groups present, e.g., ungrazed grass, bare ground with nettle, rushes, etc.

• For wet areas: indicate the water depth in June, or for temporary ponds and streams, give the period that water was present.

Estimation of Stand Characteristics

Objectives—This is a system for assessing habitat characteristics in an efficient and timely fashion at vertebrate

USDA Forest Service Gen. Tech. Rep. PSW-GTR-144-www. 1993.

37

monitoring stations. It is taken from a method developed by Bruce Bingham and C.J. Ralph.

Considerations—The information collected will provide enough data to determine the vegetation formation, association, and major structural characteristics. The types of data are those which have some logical relationship with bird requirements for feeding or nesting. The method provides enough quantitative information for correlative analyses and ordinations. It is flexible so that it can be applied to any vegetation formation, including deserts, grasslands, and forests.

Procedures—Establish a releve, a variable radius plot centered, for example, on a census point. The size of the plot will vary, depending on the homogeneity of the vegetation composition, and the density of the vegetation. Generally, this would be a radius of less than 50 m, and often about 25 m. Walk around the point for no more than 5-10 minutes, or until you stop adding new species, whichever is less. Once the search is stopped, the distance from the stopping point, or the outermost boundary of vegetation that the observer can see from the point center, is the radius of the plot and is treated as a boundary for estimating relative abundance.

If the point has more than one vegetation type, then establish two releves. An example would be along a road, with a clear cut on one side, and a mature forest on the other. No more than two releves should be established at a point.

Determine the number of major layers of vegetation within your releve by their dominant growth form: tree layer (T), shrub layer (S), herb (H), and the ground cover (moss and lichen) layer (G).

In a forest with all layers, the tree layer is the uppermost stratum, dominated by mature trees. It may be a single layer, or consist of two or more sublayers recognizable by changes in density and canopy status (see below). The shrub layer is dominated by shrubs or small trees. The herb layer is dominated by low-growing plants, typically nonwoody, although seedlings and other reproduction of trees and shrubs may be present. The ground layer is dominated by such plants as mosses, lichens, and liverworts. Bare ground and litter are ignored for this classification scheme.

We recommend the use of the following height classes for each stratum, if they are appropriate, because they can make the process less subjective. For example, the tree layer could include any plants taller than 5 m (In shorter forests, this might be lowered to 3 or 4 m, as appropriate). The shrub layer could then be established at between 50 cm to 5 m. The herb layer includes any plants less than 50 cm tall. The moss/lichen layer refers to a ground-appressed, low carpet, less than 10 cm high.

For purposes of bird-habitat association, only species of trees and shrubs need be identified and recorded in the data below. For other plants, a common name such as FERN, HERB, MOSS, or LICH will suffice for most purposes. Plant ecologists have used some species in the herb or ground cover layers as indicative of a particular plant association. In this case, the species should be recorded.

Determine the average height of each major layer present and dominant plant species. It is desirable to have additional information on structure, such as the maximum and minimum d.b.h. of canopy trees and total percent cover value of each layer.

Determine relative importance of species in each layer present. Importance can be expressed as either abundance or cover. Percent cover is probably the most common, and we suggest using it.

Below is a detailed description of the data we suggest be taken and recorded as on *figure 15*. The data are separated into Location Data and Vegetation Data.

Location Data:
State or province—The 2-column code for each.
Region—An 8-column code, designated by the investigator.
  Often, the name of the USGS quad, a prominent landmark, or a nearby town will provide the best code name.
Site data.
  • Latitude and longitude—For each point, latitude and longitude should be recorded as the southeast corner of the 1-minute block containing the point, as determined from accurate topographic maps. For example, 40°53'20"N, 124°08'45"W would be reduced to 4053-12408.
  • Elevation to nearest meter, by using an altimeter.
  • Aspect of the slope (the compass direction the observer faces when looking down hill) to the nearest degree, with a compass.
  • Percent slope, with a clinometer.
  • Presence (+) or absence (-) of water within the releve.
  • Plot radius, distance from the center to the edge of the releve.

Vegetation Data:
Vegetation Structure and Composition
  • Total cover—Estimate the cover of each of the four layers, according to the established scale such as Braun-Blanquet (Mueller-Dombois and Ellenberg 1974) or Daubenmire (1968). We recommend the Braun-Blanquet Cover Abundance Scale, which is: 5 = >75   percent cover; 4 = 50-75 percent cover; 3 = 25-50 percent cover; 2 = 5-25 percent cover; 1 = numerous, but less than 5 percent cover, or scattered, with cover up to 5 percent; + = few, with small cover; and r = rare, solitary, with small cover.
  • Height—Record to the nearest decimeter (0.1 m) the *average* height of the lower and upper bounds of each of the four layers.
  • Species—Record the species by a 4-letter code (using the first two letters of the genus and the first two of the species) with the greatest cover (foliage or crown cover) within each layer's boundary.
  • D.b.h.—For each layer where trees are present, record the diameter at breast height to the nearest centimeter of the largest tree in the layer and also for the smallest trees.
  • Species—Record the species of trees used for minimum and maximum d.b.h. measurements
  • Number of sublayers—Sublayers are useful to give the plant ecologist a quick overview of the structure of a layer, and

USDA Forest Service Gen. Tech. Rep. PSW-GTR-144-www. 1993.

are primarily relevant to the tree layer, although sometimes seen in the shrub layer. Record the number of sublayers visible in each primary layer. Record "1" if the layer is uniform and "2" or more if more than a single layer is divided into sublayers. In a primary layer, sublayers are sometimes obvious because of one or more species with shorter heights than the dominant species of the upper portion of the layer. In addition, sublayers are sometimes formed by cohorts of one or more size classes, possibly related to some event. For example, the tallest trees in a stand may form an open (low-density) layer of emergent individuals. Beneath that may be a denser layer of trees forming the main body of the tree layer. Below this denser layer may be another open or closed layer of trees that are intermediate to the main body of the canopy. This layer may consist of shade tolerant species or reproduction. Biologists should be cautioned that extreme precision is not required for this estimation, and unless sublayers are very obvious, they should not be recorded.

Species composition data

• Sublayer—For layers where sublayers have been recognized, record the sublayers with a letter designating the primary layer, followed by a number (e.g., T1, T2, T3, S1, etc.), indicating the sublayers by decreasing heights.

• Cover or cover abundance value, as above, using the Braun-Blanquet method—Because of the difficulty of determining crown covers independently for species of trees in a canopy, sometimes basal area cover of stems (trunks) has been used for tree layer species and crown cover for species in other layers. We suggest the cover abundance value for consistency.

• Species—Record the species' name for each plant species making up at least 10 percent of the cover.

Additional/optional information can be integrated into the method, if desired:

Snags: list layers with snags present; separate into those with a d.b.h. of less than 10 cm and those larger.

Logs: list those less than 10 cm diameter at large end by abundance or cover class, and those greater than 10 cm.

Comments—This type of vegetation assessment is limited by the size of the plot and the amount of estimation required. For example, a plot of even 50 m in radius obviously does not include all vegetation inhabited by birds heard or seen from a census point. This would require a plot of 200 m or more radius. However, most birds detected at a point are within 100 m, and many are within 50 m. Further, time limitations would require much more time spent monitoring vegetation than spent counting birds.

When observers are required to estimate, a substantial amount of error is introduced. What effect the degree of observer error likely with estimation would have on conclusions should be established. The principal source of error in this method of vegetation assessment is the determination of percent cover and heights. Intensive training can moderate this source of error, enabling each vegetation assessment to be placed into at least broad categories or plant associations.

Weather Monitoring

We suggest the following weather measurements three times per day, at the beginning, midpoint, and end of the census or capture period in a day. The maximum high and low temperature from each 24-hr period should also be recorded. Data from nearby weather stations may also be used. However, some measurements from the immediate area are more valuable.

• Weather—Use RAIN, DRIZZLE, SLEET, SNOW, or FOG. (If it is raining and foggy, put down RAIN.) If the above conditions do not apply, use: OVC (overcast), more than 90 percent cloud cover over entire sky; BRK (broken), 50-90 percent cloud cover; SCT (scattered), 10-50 percent cloud cover; or CLR (clear), less than 10 percent cloud cover.

• Wind Direction—Using an anemometer, stand facing into the wind and record the direction to the nearest 1/16th of the compass, i.e., N, NNE, NE, etc. If winds are variable, record predominate direction.

• Wind Speed—Record both the average and maximum speeds.

• Visibility—Estimate visibility to the nearest 250 m if less than 2 km, otherwise to the nearest kilometer.

• Barometric pressure.

• Temperature—Dry bulb temperature. Record to the nearest 1 degree centigrade.

• Relative humidity.

• Rain—Record from a rain gauge to nearest 0.1 mm.

We suggest a continuous strip chart recorder to measure temperature and a somewhat permanent station to measure rainfall.

References

Ambrose, S. 1989. **The Australian bird count—Have we got your numbers?** RAOU Newsletter, Published by the Royal Australasian Ornithologists Union, Moonee Ponds, Vic. 3039, Australia. 80:1-2.

Baillie, S.R.; Green, R.E.; Boddy, M.; Buckland, S.T. 1986. **An evaluation of the Constant Efforts Sites Scheme.** Report of the Constant Effort Sites Review Group to the Ringing Committee of the British Trust for Ornithology. British Trust for Ornithology, Beech Grove, Tring, Herts. HP23 5NR United Kingdom: [Copies are available for copying costs from the BTO, or the authors of this handbook.]

Baillie, S.; Holden, B. 1988. **Population changes on constant effort sites 1986-1987.** BTO (British Trust for Ornithology) News 155: 8-9.

Baldwin, S.P. 1931. **Bird banding by systematic trapping.** Scientific Publication Cleveland Museum of Natural History I (5): 125-168.

Baldwin, S.P.; Oberholser, H.C.; Worley, L.G. 1931. **Measurements of birds.** Scientific Publication Cleveland Museum of Natural History II.

Bart, Jonathan. 1977. **Impact of human visitations on avian nesting success.** Living Bird 16:187-192.

Bart, Jonathan; Robson, D.S. 1982. **Estimating survivorship when the subjects are visited periodically.** Ecology 63(4): 1078-1090.

Berthold, P.; Scherner, R. 1975. **Das "Mettnau-Reit-Illmitz- Programm", ein langfristiges Vogelfangprogramm der Vogelwarte Radolfzell mit vielfaltiger Fragestellung.** Vogelwarte 28:97-123.

Blake, C. 1963. **The brood patch.** Eastern Bird Banding Association Workshop Manual, 2:8-9.

Bleitz, D. 1957. **On the use of mist nets.** News from the Bird-Banders (Western Bird-banding Association) 32:22-25.

USDA Forest Service Gen. Tech. Rep. PSW-GTR-144-www. 1993.

39

Bleitz, D. 1970. **Mist nets and their use.** Inland Bird Banding News 42(2). [Available at no cost from Avinet, P.O. Box 1103, Dryden, NY 13053].

Bub, H. 1991. **Bird trapping and bird banding.** Ithaca, NY: Cornell University Press; 330 pp.

Burley, N. 1980. **Clutch overlap and clutch size: alternative and complementary reproductive tactics.** American Naturalist 115: 223-246.

CWSS and USFWS (Canadian Wildlife Service and U.S. Fish and Wildlife Service). 1991. North American bird banding. U.S. Department of Interior, Fish and Wildlife Service, Laurel, MD; and Ottawa, Canada: Environment Canada, Canadian Wildlife Service.

Conner, Richard N. 1990. **The effect of observer variability on the MacArthur foliage density estimate.** Wilson Bulletin 102: 341-343.

Conner, Richard N.; O'Halloran, Kathleen A. 1986. **A comparison of the MacArthur foliage density estimate with actual leaf surface area and biomass.** Southwestern Naturalist 31: 270-273.

Cooperrider, Allen Y.; Boyd, Raymond J.; Stuart, Hanson R. 1986. **Inventory and monitoring of wildlife habitat.** Denver, CO: Service Center, Bureau of Land Management, U.S. Department of Interior; 858 pp. [Available from the Superintendent of Documents, U.S. Government Printing Office, Washington, DC 20402; GPO # 024-011-00170-1].

Daubenmire, R.F. 1968. **Plant communities: textbook of plant synecology.** New York, NY: Harper and Row; 300 p.

DeSante, David F. 1991. **The Monitoring Avian Productivity and Survivorship (MAPS) program: first annual report.** The Institute for Bird Populations, Inverness, CA [available from IBP at P.O. Box 1346, Point Reyes Station, CA 94956].

DeSante, David F. 1992a. **Monitoring Avian Productivity and Survivorship (MAPS): a sharp, rather than blunt, tool for monitoring and assessing landbird populations.** In: McCullough, Dale R.; Barrett, Reginald H., editors. Wildlife 2001: Populations. London, UK.: Elsevier Applied Science; 511-521.

DeSante, David F. 1992b. **An invitation and instructions for participation in the Monitoring Avian Productivity (MAPS) program.** Institute for Bird Populations, P.O. Box 1346, Point Reyes Station, CA 94956.

DeSante, David F.; Geupel, Geoffrey R. 1987. **Landbird productivity in central coastal California: the relationship to annual rainfall, and a reproductive failure in 1986.** Condor 89:636-653.

Geupel, Geoffrey R.; DeSante, David F. 1990a. **Incidence and determinants of double brooding in Wrentits.** Condor 92: 67-75.

Geupel, Geoffrey R.; DeSante, David F. 1990b. **The Palomarin Handbook.** Stinson Beach, CA: Point Reyes Bird Observatory.

Ginn, H.B.; Melville, D.S. 1983. **Moult in birds.** BTO Guide 19. Hertfordshire, England: British Trust for Ornithology; 112 p.

Gottfried, Bradley M.; Thompson, Charles F. 1978. **Experimental analysis of nest predation in an old-field habitat.** Auk 95: 304-312.

Herman, S.G. 1989. **The naturalist field journal, based on the method by J. Grinnell.** Vermillion, SD: Buteo Books.

Higgins, Kenneth F.; Kirsch, Leo M.; Ball, I. Joseph, Jr. 1969. **A cable-chain device for locating duck nests.** Journal of Wildlife Management 33: 1009-1011.

Hilden, Olavi; Koskimies, Pertii; Pakarinen, Raimo; Vaisanen, Risto A. 1991. **Point count of breeding landbirds.** In: Koskimies, Pertii; Vaisanen, Risto A., editors. Monitoring bird populations. Helsinki: Zoological Museum, Finnish Museum of Natural History, University of Helsinki; 27-32.

Huff, Mark H.; Manuwal, David A.; Putera, Judy A. 1991. **Winter bird communities in the southern Washington Cascade Range.** In: Wildlife and vegetation of unmanaged Douglas-fir forests. Portland, OR: Pacific Northwest Research Station, Forest Service, U.S. Department of Agriculture; Gen. Tech. Rep. PNW-285. 533 p.

Hutchinson, G.E. 1978. **An introduction to population ecology.** New Haven, CT: Yale University Press.

I.B.C.C. (International Bird Census Committee). 1970. **An international standard for a mapping method in bird census work recommended by the International Bird Census Committee.** Audubon Field Notes 24: 722-726.

James, F.C.; Shugart, H.H., Jr. 1970. **A quantitative method of habitat description.** Audubon Field Notes 24: 727-736.

Karr, James R. 1981. **Surveying birds with mist nets.** In: Ralph, C. John; Scott, J. Michael, eds. Estimating numbers of terrestrial birds. Studies in Avian Biology 6: 62-67.

Kendeigh, S. C. 1952. **Parental care and its evolution in birds.** Illinois Biological Monograph 22: 1-357.

Kepler, Cameron B.; Scott, J. Michael. 1981. **Reducing bird count variability by training observers.** In: Ralph, C. John; Scott, J. Michael, eds. Estimating numbers of terrestrial birds. Studies in Avian Biology 6: 366-371.

Keyes, B.E.; Grue C.E. 1982. **Capturing birds with mist nets: a review.** North American Bird Bander 7(1): 2-14.

Koskimies, Pertii; Vaisanen, Risto A. 1991. **Monitoring bird populations.** Helsinki: Zoological Museum, Finnish Museum of Natural History, University of Helsinki. 145 p. (Available from Natural History Book Service, 2 Wills Rd., Totnes, Devon TQ9 5XN, United Kingdom; or St. Ann's Books, 26 Priory Rd., Great Malvern, Worcs., WR14 3DR, U.K.)

Labisky, R.F. 1957. **Relation of hay harvesting to duck nesting under a refuge-permittee system.** Journal of Wildlife Management 21: 194-200.

Lack, David. 1954. **The natural regulation of animal numbers.** London: Oxford University Press.

Lack, David. 1966. **Population studies of birds.** Oxford: Clarendon Press.

Lincoln, F.C. 1947. **Manual for bird banders.** Rev. Edition. Washington, DC: U.S. Fish and Wildlife Service.

Lincoln, F.C.; Baldwin, S.P. 1929. **Manual for bird banders.** Miscl. Publ. No. 58. Washington, DC: U.S. Department of Agriculture.

Lockley, R.M.; Russell, R. 1953. **Bird-ringing: The art of bird study by individual marking.** London: Crosby Lockwood & Son Ltd.

Low, S.H. 1957. **Banding with mist nets.** Bird-banding 28: 115-128.

Lyon, Bruce E.; Montgomerie, Robert D. 1987. **Ecological correlates of incubation feeding: a comparative study of high arctic finches.** Ecology 68(3): 713-722.

MacArthur, Robert H.; MacArthur, John W. 1961. **On bird species diversity.** Ecology 42:594-598.

Major, Richard E. 1989. **The effect of human observers on the intensity of nest predation.** Ibis 132(4): 608-612.

Manuwal, David A.; Huff, Mark. 1987. **Spring and winter bird populations in a Douglas-fir forest sere.** Journal of Wildlife Management 51(3): 586-595.

Martin, Thomas E. 1992. **Breeding productivity considerations: What are the appropriate habitat features for management?** In: Hagan, J.M.; Johnston, D.W., eds. Ecology and conservation of neotropical migrant birds. Washington, D.C.: Smithsonian Institute Press; 455-473.

Martin, Thomas E.; Geupel, Geoffrey R. **Nest-monitoring plots: Methods for locating nests and monitoring success.** Journal of Wildlife Management. [In press].

Martin, Thomas E.; Li, P. 1992. **Life history traits of cavity-versus open-nesting birds.** Ecology 73(2): 579-592.

Martin, Thomas E.; Roper, J.J. 1988. **Nest predation and nest site selection of a western population of the Hermit Thrush.** Condor 90: 51-57.

Mayfield, Harold F. 1961. **Nesting success calculated from exposure.** Wilson Bulletin 73: 255-261.

Mayfield, Harold F. 1975. **Suggestions for calculating nesting success.** Wilson Bulletin 87: 456-466.

McClure, H.E. 1984. **Bird banding.** Pacific Grove, CA: The Boxwood Press, 183 Ocean View Blvd. (Available from the publisher).

McDonald, M.V.; Greenberg, R. 1991. **Nest departure calls in female songbirds.** Condor 93: 365-373.

Mueller-Dombois, D.; Ellenberg, H. 1974. **Aims and methods of vegetation ecology.** New York, NY: John Wiley and Sons, Inc. 547 p.

Noon, Barry R. 1981. **Techniques for sampling avian habitats.** In: Capen, David E., ed. The use of multivariate statistics in studies of wildlife habitat. Gen. Tech. Rep. RM-87. Forest Service, U.S. Department of Agriculture; 42-52.

Peach, Will J. 1992. **Combining mark-recapture data sets for small passerines.** Proceedings of the EURING 1992 Technical Conference.

Peach, Will J.; Baillie, Stephen. 1991. **Population changes on constant effort sites 1989-1990.** BTO (British Trust for Ornithology) News 173: 12-14.

Peach, Will J.; Baillie, Stephen; Underhill, Les. 1991. **Survival of British Sedge Warblers** *Acrocephalus schoenobaenus* **in relation to West African rainfall.** Ibis 133:300-305.

Peach, Will J.; Buckland, S.T.; Baillie, Stephen R. 1990. **Estimating survival rates using mark-recapture data from multiple ringing sites.** The Ring 13: 87-102.

Picozzi, N. 1975. **Crow predation on marked nests.** Journal of Wildlife Management 39: 151-155.

Pyle, Peter; Howell, S.N.G.; Yunick, R.P.; DeSante, David F. 1987. **Identification guide to North American passerines.** Bolinas, CA: Slate Creek Press, P.O. Box 219, 94924. (Available from publisher).

Ralph, C. John. 1967. **Taking data at a banding station.** Western Bird-banding Association Workshop Manual. Bolinas, CA: Point Reyes Bird Observatory, Bolinas, California.

Ralph, C. John. 1976. **Standardization of mist net captures for quantification of avian migration.** Bird-Banding 47: 44-47.

Ralph, C. John. 1978. **Disorientation and possible fate of young passerine coastal migrants.** Bird-Banding 49: 237-247.

Ralph, C. John. 1981a. **Age ratios and their possible use in determining autumn routes of passerine migrants.** Wilson Bulletin 93: 164-188.

Ralph, C. John. 1981b. **Terminology used in estimating numbers of birds.** In: Ralph, C. John; Scott, J. Michael, eds. Estimating numbers of terrestrial birds. Studies in Avian Biology No. 6: 577-578.

Ralph, C. John. 1988. **A brief guide to banding birds.** Western Bird-banding Association Workshop Manual. Arcata, CA: Humboldt Bay Bird Observatory.

Ralph, C. John. 1992. **In memoriam: L. Richard Mewaldt, 1917-1990.** Auk 109(3): 646-647.

Ralph, C. John; Droege, Sam; Sauer, John R. **Managing and monitoring birds using point counts: Standards and applications.** In: Ralph, C. John; Sauer, John R.; Droege, Sam, eds. Monitoring landbirds with point counts. Gen. Tech. Rep. Albany, CA: Pacific Southwest Research Station, Forest Service, U.S. Department of Agriculture. [In press].

Ralph, C. John; Scott, J. Michael, eds. 1981. **Estimating numbers of terrestrial birds.** Studies in Avian Biology No. 6. 630 p.

Ricklefs, R.E. 1969a. **An analysis of nesting mortality in birds.** Smithsonian Contributions Zoology 9: 1-48.

Ricklefs, R.E. 1969b. **The nesting cycle of songbirds in tropical and temperate regions.** Living Bird 8: 165-175.

Ricklefs, R.E.; Bloom, G. 1977. **Components of avian breeding productivity.** Auk 94: 86-96.

Robbins, Chandler S.; Bridge, D.; Feller, R. 1959. **Relative abundance of adult male redstarts at an inland and a coastal locality during fall migration.** Maryland Birdlife 15: 23-25.

Robbins, Chandler S.; Bystrak, Danny; Geissler, Paul H. 1986. **The breeding bird survey: Its first fifteen years, 1965-1979.** Resource Publication 157. Washington, DC: U.S. Department of Interior, Fish and Wildlife Service.

Robbins, Chandler S.; Sauer, John R.; Greenberg, R.S.; Droege, Sam. 1989. **Population declines in North American birds that migrate to the neotropics.** Proceedings of the National Academy of Sciences (USA) 86: 7658-7662.

Shreve, A. 1965. **Preventing net casualties.** Eastern Bird Banding Association, *Workshop Manual*, Vol. 4: 1-22.

Silver, R.; Andrews, H.; Ball, G.F. 1985. **Parental care in an ecological perspective: a quantitative analysis of avian subfamilies.** American Zoology 25: 823-840.

Slack, R.D. 1976. **Nest guarding behavior by male Gray Catbirds.** Auk 93: 292-300.

Temple, Stan A.; Wiens, J.A. 1989. **Bird populations and environmental changes: can birds be bio-indicators?** American Birds 43: 260-270.

Van Horne, B. 1983. **Density as a misleading indicator of habitat quality.** Journal of Wildlife Management 47(4): 893-901.

Verner, Jared; Milne, Kathleen A. 1989. **Coping with sources of variability when monitoring population trends.** Ann. Zool. Fennici 26: 191-200.

Verner, Jared; Morrison, Michael L.; Ralph, C. John, eds. 1986. **Wildlife 2000: Modeling habitat relationships of terrestrial vertebrates.** Madison, WI: University of Wisconsin Press. 470 pp.

Westmoreland, D.; Best, L.B. 1985. **The effect of disturbance on Mourning Dove nesting success.** Auk 102: 774-780.

Willis, E.O. 1973. **Survival rates for visited and unvisited nests of Bicolored Antbirds.** Auk 90: 263-267.

Zerba, E.; Morton, M.L. 1983. **The rhythm of incubation from egg-laying to hatching in Mountain White-crowned Sparrows.** Ornis Scandinavica 14: 188-197.

USDA Forest Service Gen. Tech. Rep. PSW-GTR-144-www. 1993.

41